CW00521942

Ayrshire needlework

Fig 1 'Motherless'. This plaster by George A. Lawson (1832–1904) in the Museum & Art Galleries, Kelvingrove, Glasgow, gives us a feeling of compassion for those who lived with the hardships and grief of the period when Ayrshire needlework, a most beautiful and technically difficult embroidery, was in its heyday

Agnes F. Bryson

Ayrshire needlework

B.T. Batsford Ltd. London

© Agnes F. Bryson 1989

First published 1989
All rights reserved. No part of this publication
may be reproduced, in any form or by any means,
without permission from the Publisher
ISBN 0 7134 5928 X (cased)

Typeset by Lasertext
and printed in Great Britain by
Bath Press, Bath
for the publishers

B. T. Batsford Ltd
4 Fitzhardinge Street
London W1H 0AH

*A CIP record for this book is available from
the British Library*

Contents

Acknowledgements

I am thankful for the gracious memories of all the wonderful women who encouraged my interest in Ayrshire needlework and took the time and trouble to pass on to me their knowledge of this beautiful old local craft. My most affectionate thanks are due to my husband for his patient help and tolerance when my thoughts were over a hundred years away and I was not the best of company. I am deeply indebted to my daughter, Oonagh Grassie, who made my drawings presentable and provided the map of Ayrshire. Without her help this book could not have been written. Special thanks also to my younger daughter, Anne Hadden, for her help with the research, and to my son Alastair for his advice in selecting the photographs and to both for their unfailing interest. My warmest thanks go to Ina Graham for the photographs and to Nan Morton for the sketches; to Maxwell Wilson for reading and correcting all my material and to Jacqui Flack for teaching me how to master my word processor. To Liz Arthur for her help and advice, especially for being so patient with a complete beginner, I offer my grateful thanks. My thanks also go to Margaret H. Swain for rekindling my interest in Ayrshire needlework; to the staff of the Dick Institute, Kilmarnock, especially Mrs Crosbie and Mrs Geddes; to Mrs Andrews, Mike Bailey and the staff at Carnegie Library and Rozelle, Ayr; and to Chrissie Clarke, Sandie Shaw, Pat Adams, Barbara Graham, Clare Stoughton-Harris and the staff of the Mitchell Library, Glasgow. To my 'Wednesday morning class' – Peggy Greer, Eithne Johnston, Catherine McAllister, Gerry McGee, Margaret Orcharton, and Ruth Robertson – go my most sincere thanks for their faith and encouragement, especially when my enthusiasm was flagging. Last, but by no means least, my appreciation goes to my editors Rachel Wright and Sandra Winfield for their help, encouragement and patience.

Agnes F. Bryson
July 1989

1 Introduction

Dream stitches

'She never cared for sewing, but it's different now, you know,

For she sits each day and stitches, and her eyes are all aglow,

As she handles each wee garment, and her glad heart sweetly sings

With a mother's love and longing as she makes those tiny things –

"I am stitching dreams my baby; many a dream and many a prayer

Will be sewn into the garments that my little one will wear.

And I think, perhaps, they'll whisper very soft to you, my dear

Of the love that has been waiting just to make you welcome here!"'

(From *Aunt Kate's Day-By-Day Book*, John Leng & Co. Ltd, 1937, p. 296)

In researching this book, my biggest problem has been sorting out the truth from the myths. Many a proud young mother has told me that her baby's robe, obviously made *c.*1820–40, was all the work of her Grandmother. There is no need to be a mathematician to work out that this is a sheer impossibility. If she had added a few Greats, she would, perhaps, have been closer to the truth. Another common mistake is for people with little knowledge of the craft to insist that their precious robe was worked about two hundred years ago, when it is actually of machine-made insertion, and of a style which was in vogue at the beginning of the twentieth century. In over thirty years of studying hundreds of robes and asking innumerable questions, I often have to suppress a chuckle at the improbable stories which have been passed down, in all innocence, with treasured heirlooms. I never have the heart to disillusion those involved.

Ayrshire needlework will probably never be worked again commercially as a viable proposition, not because of the cost of the materials used, but because of the time it takes. One handkerchief takes fifty hours or more to complete, so the cost would be prohibitive. I can only see it being worked in future years for the satisfaction of completing a piece of embroidery of outstanding artistic merit, or to produce a cherished family heirloom.

Several organisations, including the Embroiderers' Guild and the Scottish Women's Rural Institutes, have tried to keep this old craft alive by holding day schools and residential courses, and by including classes for Ayrshire needlework in their competition schedules. Mrs Limond of Minishant, a lover of and authority on Ayrshire needlework, told me of an attempt to revive it just before the first World War, but even then the needlepoint fillings, which distinguish true Ayrshire needlework from other whitework, were not worked.

A second attempt, in which I was personally involved, occurred in 1956 when Miss E. W. Thomson, Adviser in Art and Crafts to the Federation of Scottish Women's Rural Institutes (SWRI) and also a devotee of Ayrshire needlework, persuaded the Ayrshire Federation to arrange six classes, to be taught by Mrs McGinn of Irvine. I was the youngest to attend these classes, and was addicted from the very first stitch. We learned all the basic stitches in the classes, but I still had to unpick part of an old robe in order to discover how to do the more advanced work such as laddering. This revival of the craft was so popular that a class for Ayrshire needlework was included in the 1957 SWRI Federation show. The number of entries for this was much greater than anticipated.

In the following year (1958) the Royal Highland and Agricultural Society included in their schedule two classes for Ayrshire needlework in the handcrafts section of the Royal Highland Show. One class was for a handkerchief, to be worked on fine lawn using traditional stitches, and the other was for a traycloth worked on linen, also using traditional stitches. This second article is a bit misleading, as true Ayrshire needlework was never worked on table linen. The muslin or cotton lawn used is far too fine for domestic use.

About this time I read an excellent history on Ayrshire needlework – *The Flowerers*, by M. H. Swain, published by W. & R. Chambers Ltd., London and Edinburgh. In the last chapter, Mrs Swain states, 'it [Ayrshire needlework] was born and died at the whim of fashion'.

Living in Ayrshire, surrounded by all the towns and villages where Ayrshire needlework had once been a thriving industry, I felt I could not allow this beautiful old craft to die. I therefore set myself the task of keeping it alive and passing on my knowledge of it to as many people as possible.

Obtaining materials was a problem at first, as the fine white cotton lawn required for Ayrshire needlework was no longer available. I struggled on, buying any old fine white material that I could find in Oxfam, plain white handkerchiefs, and Architect's linen (from which I had to bleach out the drawings).

Several suppliers now stock a good quality cotton lawn, but as the sheer muslin used in the nineteenth century is no longer produced, many of the original needlelace stitches cannot be worked effectively. On the weight of material now available their effect is completely lost.

Most modern sewing threads are either mercerised or synthetic, and have a sheen, which means they will not give an authentic finish. I experimented with different brands and weights of thread, and found that an ordinary cotton sewing thread was the most successful.

For many years I worked on my own, entering competitions to try to bring Ayrshire needlework to the notice of the public, giving talks and taking classes at every opportunity. Several of these classes were for Americans, who had discovered the craft and were fascinated by it. I have taught all over Britain and in Canada, and I have also given lessons to many students in my home.

No art offers greater scope for perception and ingenuity than embroidery, and Ayrshire needlework offers more than most other types. The stitches used are basic, simple ones – satin, stem, blanket, etc. – but it is the variety of ways in which they are used which builds this style of needlework up into a work of art. Technically, it ranks higher than any other embroidery.

The first hurdle the embroiderer has to overcome is keeping the work small, but this is easily mastered with practice. It is like knitting: you have to get the tension right. If I have not done any work for some time, I always work a few stitches on a scrap of material before I take up the piece I am working on. Many of my students have found this a useful suggestion.

I hope this book will encourage the reader to take up the fine needle and thread and work an heirloom which will be increasingly treasured by your family for generations to come. What a pride and joy there is in having your work admired by all the guests at a christening. A friend's baby becomes even more precious if wearing a robe made by you with love and patience, for patience is the main ingredient in Ayrshire needlework. The lovely old Scottish custom of lending out a beautiful and cherished robe still remains.

Fig 2 Map of Ayrshire

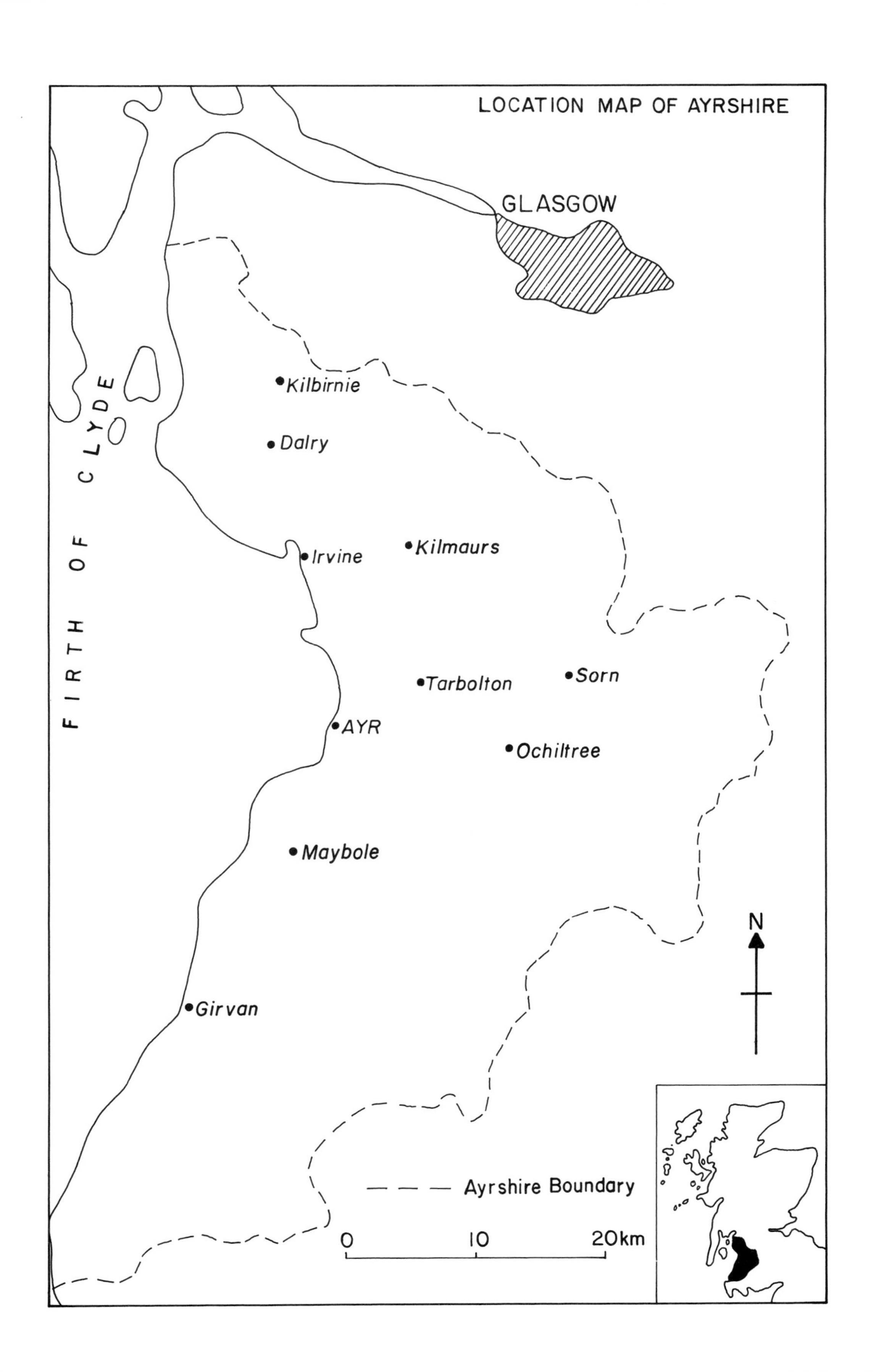
LOCATION MAP OF AYRSHIRE
GLASGOW
FIRTH OF CLYDE
Kilbirnie
Dalry
Irvine
Kilmaurs
Tarbolton
Sorn
AYR
Ochiltree
Maybole
Girvan
N
Ayrshire Boundary
0
10
20km

2 A legend of Ayrshire white needlework

Imagine a scene many hundreds of years ago, when Saint Kentigern, while on a pastoral mission to Strathclyde (of which Ayrshire is part), came suddenly upon the hideous aftermath of a battle: the murdered bodies of many young children and naked women, the victims of rape. Men and youths had also not been spared.

He spent the day burying the dead, and in the evening sought shelter in a cave; but it was no ordinary cave, for it was filled with a brilliant light. On an altar there lay a baby, dressed in a soft fair robe and bonnet which were glistening white and of exceeding fineness, which no mortal fingers could weave, with embellishment like samite (rich thread embroidery of great beauty). The baby turned and smiled at him. He knelt before it, and spent the night in worship and adoration. During the hours of darkness was revealed to him much which is usually only reserved for the hereafter.

In the morning when he rose he found the baby gone, but left behind where it had lain, folded in a mystical fashion, was the robe with the little bonnet on top of it. Saint Kentigern immediately set to work building a chapel, in which he gave the robe and bonnet pride of place. Many mothers came from afar to worship and admire this symbol of motherhood.

This is a simplified version of 'A Legend of Ayrshire White Needlework', as told by James A. Morris, ARSA FRIBA in *The Art of Ayrshire White Needlework*, Begg, Currie & Russell, Glasgow 1916.

'Saint Kentigern, better known as Saint Mungo, became patron saint of Glasgow and on the spot where he built his little wooden chapel now stands Glasgow Cathedral.'
The People's History of Glasgow by John K. McDowall, published in Glasgow and London in 1899.

3 The social background

To understand the conditions under which this most beautiful and technically difficult embroidery was worked in its heyday, we must transport ourselves back to the beginning of the nineteenth century.

The people of Ayrshire were a tough, hardy race. If they survived the rigours of childhood, they usually lived to a ripe old age. This can be observed on many of the tombstones in local graveyards. Sometimes whole families of four or five children could die within a few months, and yet their parents would survive to live well into their eighties or nineties.

They had a very *pawky* sense of humour, which must have helped them overcome the repressions and hardships of the time. The roads were just rough tracks, called 'Kirk' or 'coffin' roads because they were mainly used for going to church or to funerals, which, like baptisms, were steeped in custom and involved the whole community. There was no piped water, electricity, or means of communication by telephone, and potatoes and oatmeal were the staple diet. The thatched homes were mere hovels, with a peat-burning hearth or an open fireplace in the middle of the room. The floors were of earth and the dung-heap was at the door, yet under these conditions the women were able to produce some of the most technically difficult and exquisite embroideries in existence today.

A lot of the women had trouble with their eyes, and this may have been exacerbated by the dull light inside the cottages and the peat fumes. In *The Art of Ayrshire White Needlework*, James A. Morris states that the older women bathed their eyes with whisky to sharpen their eyesight. In order to confirm or disprove this, I tried it and, although I would not recommend it, I did not find the experiment nearly as painful as I had expected. After the initial sting the effect was quite soothing, but my eyesight was neither sharpened nor improved in any way.

One room in the house contained the handloom. This was originally for the production of woollen material but, with the change in fashion, was later used to weave cotton, which was much cheaper to produce, easier to launder and did not shrink. This room was recognisable from the outside of the house as it had two windows, to give maximum light, as against one in the living

Fig 3 Jougs

area. Attached to the living quarters was the byre for the cattle, which provided extra warmth in winter.

The Church greatly influenced the community, and was itself, in turn, under the jurisdiction of the local landowner. The Landlord and the Minister reigned supreme: their word was law, and today we can appreciate but little of the fear these righteous gentlemen caused ordinary men and women.

The 'jougs', still in use for small offences, were a much dreaded punishment. They consist of an iron collar about six inches in diameter, made of two semi-circular pieces linked together at one end and made sure with a padlock at the other. They are attached to a chain of six links, the upper end of which is fixed to the church wall, about seven feet from the ground. The collar was placed around the neck of the offender, the padlock made fast, and he or she stood in humility before his or her peers, who threw at him or her all the rubbish which could be found. Local folklore tells of one woman, a webster (weaver), who was ordered to be fined, to be placed in the jougs from 11 am to 12 noon for one week, and on the following Sabbath to stand in front of the congregation, confess to swearing, cursing and fighting with her mother-in-law, to declare her repentance and to promise never to do these things again. A similar punishment was meted out to another webster for weaving on a Sunday.

Should some hapless, unmarried girl become pregnant, she and her lover had to sit both dressed in sackcloth on low stools, in church on four consecutive Sundays, and to confess to her sins. The embarrassment of this punishment caused some of these mentally tortured and very unhappy girls to conceal their pregnancies, which in turn led to their being prosecuted for intent to murder their new-born babies. This was the cause of many suicides.

The jougs still exist at my own church in Fenwick, but today are used only as a threat to naughty children and to appear in many wedding photograph albums, where a smiling bride or groom is seen posing, firmly secured, while the guests busy themselves with their cameras.

In contrast, babies born in wedlock were taken to the hearts of everyone in the villages. The women would get together to make the layette, including beautifully embroidered day dresses and bonnets. Because the houses were so cold and draughty, babies had to wear bonnets indoors, day and night. Those worn during the night were not embroidered, and were made of either flannel or linen cambric. If the mother or a close relative of a baby died, black ribbons were attached to his or her bonnet during the period of mourning.

Births and baptisms were surrounded by mystery and tradition. Pregnancy and childbirth were still treated as illness. During the third or fourth week after her baby's birth, the mother would invite all her acquaintances and relations to visit her on the day she had chosen to show off her new child. It was the custom for her to sit fully clothed on a bed made up with an embroidered white cover and pillows. It would have been considered indecent for her to receive people in her nightclothes. The visitors all drank wine and ate cake – this was called 'wetting the baby's head'. It was usually a disgrace for a woman to be seen drunk, but on this happy occasion it was apparently quite permissible.

The same company was invited to the christening, at which all the women sat together in the kirk (church), and then walked in a bang (crowd) to the child's home for a blithmeat (banquet). Each woman took with her some food, such as a loaf of bread. The baby had to be carried by a young unmarried woman, who held in her hand a piece of bread and cheese and a preen (pin) used in the making of the baby's dress. This was called a 'christening piece', and she had to

Fig 4 The inside of a little nightcap showing the strings which were drawn up and tied to mould it into the shape of the baby's head. By using this method a bonnet could be made to fit a child from new-born to three years. The string is very hard, so it must have been most uncomfortable for the baby wearing it. To prevent choking, these little bonnets were never tied under the chin (Author's collection)

present it to the first man she met. On one occasion this happened to be a young English nobleman who knew nothing of the custom, who, after remonstrating with the girl and denying any knowledge of her or her child, announced that he was an Earl. 'Though you were a King on a throne Sir, ye maun tak' this bread and cheese', she is said to have implored. There are different versions of this custom, such as giving the christening piece to a man if the baby is a girl and to a woman if a boy, but in Ayrshire it was always presented to a man regardless of the child's sex. Another custom carried out at a blithmeat was to pass the baby three times around the fire to ward off evil spirits.

'Shortnin', or Shortening Day, was yet another special day in a baby's life. When the baby was four or five months old, he or she was promoted to short clothes, which was another excuse for the friends and relations of the parents to gather for refreshments, and to admire and congratulate. This custom was apparently continued into the early twentieth century.

4 The barefoot boy

I like this charming story about a little barefoot boy, which gives us a sympathy for the quality of life in these hard times.

> When James [Brown] was about the age of ten his father, who by that time had been promoted to be overseer of a pit, fell seriously ill with rheumatic fever, and was off work for several months. This meant a severe drain on the family exchequer, and Mrs Brown found it necessary to supplement their meagre finances. Before her marriage she had been an expert hand-sewer with a special aptitude for what was known as 'Flowering' on baptismal robes and other articles. In resuming her old occupation she found ready employment by means of many commissions from a ware-room in Tarbolton. It was the task of James to carry the completed work to Tarbolton and obtain fresh material for the next job, along with payment for what had been done. It meant a journey of seven miles on foot each time, but he found this no great hardship, and there was always a penny for biscuits on the way, which he often spent instead on whipcord for spinning his 'peerie' [top]. One day the Rev. David Ritchie, of Tarbolton, was driving along the road in his dog-cart, and James ran alongside for more than a mile. While the pony was being allowed to walk up a hill, Mr Ritchie got into conversation with the boy who was still alongside, and learned something of his history and the errand on which he was engaged. 'And can your mother trust you to carry back the money?' asked the minister. 'Oh aye', was the proud reply. In due course of further talk Mr Ritchie learned of the penny the boy received for each message and of the purchase of whipcord. 'If I gave you sixpence,' he said, 'it would buy a lot. Would you spend it on whipcord?' 'No, sir,' was the prompt reply, 'I would give it to my mother.' 'Well here's sixpence for you,' said the minister, and before they drove off, Miss Ritchie leaned out of the dog-cart to pat the boy on the head, and as she did so, she slipped another sixpence into his hand. To this day Mr Brown declares, 'I am sure there was not a prouder boy in all the parish, nor a prouder mother, when I placed the two sixpences in her hand that day.'

Taken from *From Pit to Palace*, by Alexander Gammie, published by James Clark & Co. Ltd., 9 Essex St., Strand, London WC2 in 1931. The barefoot boy became the Hon. James Brown MP, Lord High Commissioner to the General Assembly of the Church of Scotland.

5 A bride's providin' (Dower Chest) in the 1840s

This contained the following items:

A chest of drawers, which had to be new, and ordered for the purpose
Bed and table linen
Woven blankets
Silver spoons
A clock
A ladle
Candles and stick
Dookin' goon (Ducking gown – Ayrshire for baptismal robe), with handwork
A cutty sark (short nightdress worn in childbirth)

This list was given to me in the 1930s by an eighty-year-old lady as the requirements her mother was expected to have collected before she could contemplate marriage. Her wedding took place on 21 August 1846. The candles would be homemade; the ladle was to show that she had some experience of cooking. I find this list rather amusing, particularly the silver spoons at a time when life was so frugal. It also shows that a christening robe was part of a girl's 'bottom drawer'. Embroidered gowns were worn as day or 'best' dresses, and some infants had more than one. When I was a child there were two in my home, and I used them to dress my kittens and puppies when I pushed them around in my doll's pram, ignorant of the love, hopes and patience which must have gone into the execution of these robes. Many of the old robes are patched and darned, and show signs of a great deal of wear which they could not have acquired if they had only been used for baptisms. Soon after her marriage a bride was expected to make her 'winding sheet' (shroud), which was perhaps thought necessary because of the number of young women who died in childbirth.

6 Ayrshire needlework

Ayrshire needlework, white muslin or cotton lawn, embroidered with a white cotton thread and used mainly on articles of clothing, was known locally as 'sewed muslin', 'floo'erin' (flowering) or 'spriggin' (sprigging), as the designs worked were derived exclusively from nature. 'Ayrshire needlework' is the correct name for this technique. It is only since the beginning of the twentieth century that the names 'Ayrshire whitework', 'Ayrshire embroidery', 'Ayrshire lace' and, more recently, just 'Ayrshire', have been used. It should not be confused with tambouring, which is a completely different technique worked with a tambour hook over a frame. Ayrshire needlework is worked freehand, although a small sewing ring or hoop will facilitate the working of the needlepoint, drawn thread, and drawn fabric fillings.

In the beginning, as with all good craftwork, the design and embroidery were executed by the same person, but as the industry became more commercialised the women worked on stamped material delivered to them by agents or packmen from the warehouses. During the summer months the women worked outside their homes, sitting on Floo'erin Stanes (flowering stones) – large stones covered with a turf or straw for added comfort. These were placed where they caught most light, usually in front of the cottages, and often arranged in a row in front of one house so that the workers could gossip as they

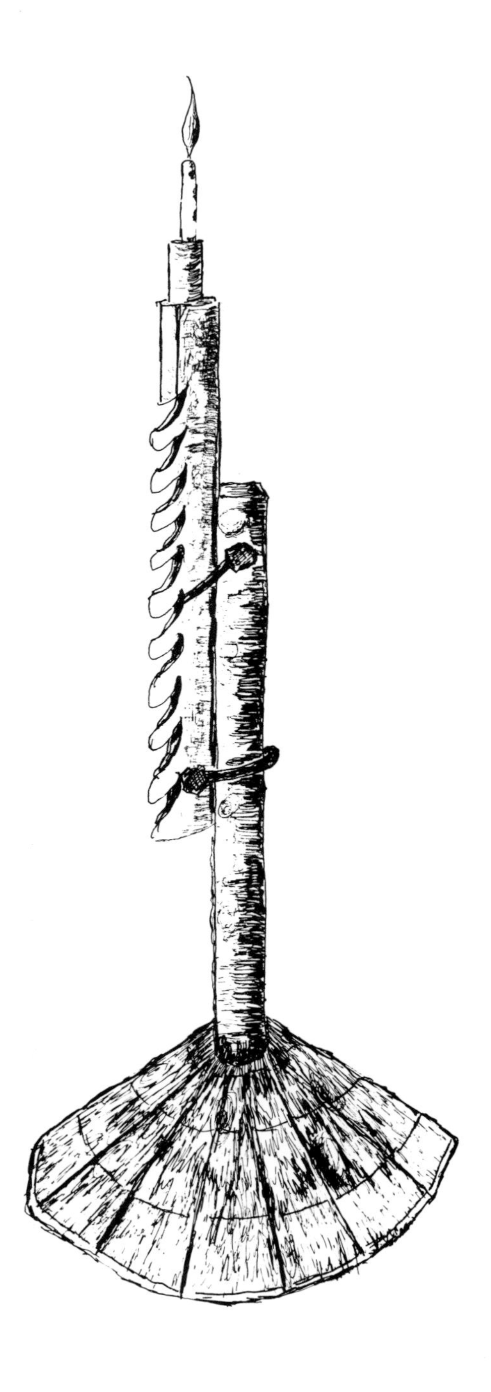

Fig 5 A 'puir man'. Many elegant turned wood examples of these candle holders can be seen in houses open to the public throughout Scotland. The Flowerers' candlestick was a very crude, homemade affair from roughly hewn wood. A description of the 'puir man' is given in *The Concise Scots Dictionary* (Aberdeen University Press)

worked. In this way the work could be passed from 'Flowerer' to 'Flowerer', so that each could work the stitches at which she excelled. By this method, the standard of work was kept very high, as the technique of Ayrshire needlework can be mastered only by a great deal of practice. In the evenings the work was done by the light from a fire burning cannel coal (a type of coal which gives off a very bright flame) or a candle in a candlestick about a metre high which had a ratchet so that it could be raised or lowered depending on the number of women working around it.

The candlestick was called a 'puir man' (poor man). This name derived from the time when a pine log full of resin was cut into strips about one inch square and two feet long, and burned like a candle. It was the duty of the younger members of the family to take charge of these 'wooden candles', but if a beggar came into the home and received food and shelter he was expected, in return for this hospitality, to replenish and hold these primitive tapers. When a permanent stand was invented, 'puir man' was the name given to it. These old candlesticks have all disappeared. I expect that when her candlestick became redundant, the prudent Flowerer chopped it up and piled it on the fire, to get the benefit of the warmth from the extra firewood.

Three months were allowed in which to learn the techniques, during which time the apprentice received very little or no remuneration. The needlepoint fillings were worked by the most experienced embroideresses after the solid parts of the work had been completed. They received a higher rate of pay for this specialised work.

After the embroidery had been completed, it had to be laundered before it was sent to a warehouse to be cut from the foundation material, made up and prepared for sale.

Ayrshire needlework originated as a truly local craft. The women of Ayrshire, particularly those in the rural areas, always spent the 'forenichts' (evenings) spinning yarn (span lint), which they sold on market days to help eke out their meagre incomes. These women were approached by Mrs Jamieson, the wife of an Ayr cotton agent, and taught a new type of embroidery (Ayrshire needlework) which she had devised as a result of studying a robe brought back from France by Lady Mary Montgomerie, heiress to the Earl of Eglinton. Mrs Jamieson was an excellent organiser and strict disciplinarian. She would not tolerate poor workmanship, and the time schedule worked out for each piece had to be adhered to (see Fig 13). It was Mrs Jamieson and her daughters who had the insight and ingenuity to organise these women into the flourishing industry which Ayrshire needlework became. This can be seen from the Statistical Accounts of the needlework trade in Ayrshire. Eighty thousand women were estimated at one time to have been employed in flowering.

Some contemporary accounts are given below:

> A species of trade peculiar to Ayrshire, not generally known, although its effects are felt by hundreds of spinsters in Ayr and elsewhere, is the manufacture of Ayrshire Needlework, in the form of robes, capes and handkerchiefs etc. etc., which are prepared in this town and neighbourhood, in consequence of orders from Glasgow, Edinburgh, London, Dublin and even America and the Continent. This wonderful work has arrived at great perfection, and orders in Ayr are executed by
>
> Mrs Jamieson — Mrs Maitland
> Mrs Williamson — Mrs McCarter
> Mrs Donald — and others
>
> For giving out of webs (sewing)
>
> Mrs Cowan — Mrs Gibson, Whitletts
> Miss Mary Logan — Miss Reid
> Mr Q. Dalrymple — Mrs Beaton

(*McCarter Directory of Ayr*, 1830)

> The Ayrshire Needlework employs not less than perhaps 600–700 hands, principally young girls, and the produce besides home consumpt, is carried to all parts of the world.

(*McCarter Directory of Ayr*, 1832)

The auld toon o'Ayr

There was a kind of work called Ayrshire Needlework, which had its origin here, gave extensive employment to females, and was in great demand for many years, but in course of time, tambouring and machinery drove it out of the market and any sewing that is now done is most miserably paid. So long as the demand lasted it gave support to many families; and many a scanty income of the more respectable was largely supplemented by it. The flowering and pointing of muslin was carried on to a great extent by agents commissioned from Glasgow, and proved a great blessing to many females in this community. About 300 in this parish were thus employed, and earned from 4d to 2s per day.

(Henry C. Gray, 1872. No publisher, but all proceeds from this book to go to Ayr Public Libraries)

7 Statistical accounts

Newton-upon-Ayr

It can be estimated, there are 600 to 700 women, principally girls and unmarried women, employed in hand-sewing for warehouses in Glasgow. The Ayrshire needlework, so extensively known and justly celebrated, was executed in this parish forty years ago and it has been gradually improving until the present day. It consists of various patterns sewed on muslin and cambric for ladies' dresses, babies' robes, caps, etc. From the year 1815 when point was introduced into the work, the demand for it in London and other parts of England, as well as in Dublin and Edinburgh, has increased to a considerable extent. It is also sent to France, Russia and Germany, and is exposed for sale in the shops of Paris. This valuable means of employment affords a fair profit to the manufacturer, and gives support to many respectable females, who by dint of industry, can earn from 1s to 1s 6d and in some cases 2s per day. In this work, which is confined to Ayr and its neighbourhood, several hundreds are engaged: and it is calculated that at least from 50 to 60 of them, who are chiefly young women, reside in the parish of Newton.

Auchinleck

A number of women, both older and younger, throughout the parish, are engaged in flowering of muslin. This is not confined to those residing in the village, but many of the farmers' daughters and others find it a profitable employment. The cloth is sent out by Glasgow houses, to their several agents in the country, who take the charge of getting it flowered and returning it. The whole of the work is done by the needle, and is therefore very tedious, but so expert have those occupied in it become, that Ayrshire work is considered superior, and brings a higher price in the market. The wages earned in this way are from 5s to 8s weekly, and sometimes considerably more.

Riccarton

A great proportion of the females in the parish are employed in sewing and embroidering muslin. Their wages vary from 9d to 3s 6d per week; but this latter sum can only be earned at the best work, and by the most expert sewers, and at expense of comfort to themselves. The employment, we believe, is very injurious to the general health of those so employed, but especially to their chest and eyes.

Ochiltree

A considerable number of young females in the village, and in some parts of the country, are employed in sewing muslin – an employment which in most cases unfits them for other occupations, and, besides, it frequently injures their health, and leaves them very helpless when they get houses of their own, as to the management of their domestic concerns.

Sorn

The rapid increase in the population from 1775 to 1831, arose from the establishment of the cotton manufactory, and the decrease from 1836 has arisen chiefly from the improvements which have taken place in machinery, by means of which in some establishments, fewer persons are required. In the cotton manufactory and bleachfield 913 persons are employed, 315 males and 598 females. Also in the village are 100 hand sewers; 3 sewing mistresses; 6 cloth merchants; and 5 white seam sewers.

Torbolton (Tarbolton)

At present [1845], the number of occupied looms is 140. The work is all got from Glasgow. It gives considerable circulation of money to the place. At the same time, it is to be lamented, that the hand-loom weavers are often unable to earn adequate wages. There are only a very few looms employed at customer or house-hold work. Domestic manufacture, to a great extent, is discontinued, and a large proportion of the females, both of the village and the county, have laid aside the spinning-wheel, and are employed at sowed [sic] work. The Ayrshire work is beautifully executed here, and is the chief source of support to many families.

Kilmaurs

200 to 300 women are gainfully employed in floo'erin muslin webs provided by agents from Girvan and Maybole.

Dalry

A large number of females in the parish are employed sewing and embroidering Ayrshire needlework for the Glasgow and Paisley markets. A good sewer may earn 1d each hour at ordinary white work. For a short period during Summer when embroidery is brisk, 1s 6d to 2s per day is occasionally earned at a fourteen to sixteen hours' sitting. But this is gained at a probable sacrifice of health.

Kilbirnie

There are 150 females employed by agents for Glasgow and Paisley houses, in sprigging or flowering muslin. This branch of industry is very well paid at present, as, without any outlay or much broken time, an expert and diligent sewer will earn from 7s to 10s a week, though probably the average gains, one with another, throughout the year, do not exceed 1s per day. This employment furnishes the means of decent support to many respectable females, and is decidedly preferred by nearly all the young women, natives of Kilbirnie, to working in either the manufactory or on the farms.

Irvine

The number of women engaged in ornamental needle-work, may amount to nearly 2000. While learning their art, these persons make very little, but when they become expert workers, they will earn from 10d to 1s 4d per day; and the length of their day, in general, is from seven in the morning to eleven or twelve at night.

(*The New Statistical Account of Scotland, Vol. V Ayr and Bute*, William Blackwood & Sons, Edinburgh & London, 1845)

8 Tools and embroideries of the nineteenth century

(All dates are approximate)

Fig. 6 shows a renovated measuring tape and pincushion in 'Mauchline Ware', which was also a thriving industry in Ayrshire from 1810 and, like Ayrshire needlework, is now becoming very collectable. The embroidery rings shown are of brass and may have been made by a husband, father or friend who worked in one of the brass foundries in the area. When I first used these rings as shown in the photograph, I was very disappointed to find that they were useless in practice as they did not fit closely together. When, however, I bound them with thin scraps of material, they were transformed. Because of their depth, they keep the material beautifully taut and are easy to control in use. I wonder if the original owner also bound them?

Scissors were small, but note the very slim blades with sharp points, which were essential when working this type of embroidery. The needles are *c.* 1840–50, and are the same as those used by the 'Flowerers'. They were on sale locally during the heyday of the 'flowering'. French Superfine 'y' quality are reputed to be the best needles ever produced. The small 'y' marked just under the eye indicates absolute top quality.

The stilettos in Fig 7 are of bone and bone with steel; one, shown second from the right, is bone with brass. The two very small ones joined by a cord are worn round the neck. I find this is an excellent idea, as I keep mislaying my single one and waste precious time looking for it. These are the only joined stilettos I have seen. The top bodkin is *c.* 1820, and has two 'eyes': one for tape and a smaller one for string or the very fine tape (2 mm wide), which was used to secure the early robes and bonnets. Bodkins were used to thread the tape or string through tucks or a casing of material. The knob on the end was to prevent it from piercing the material as it was threaded through. The middle example is stamped 'Neweys Wizard Patented'.

The paper sampler of edgings and insertions in Fig 8 is of the type shown to the customer. She would choose her pattern from this, and have it worked on commission. Although the sampler is *c.* 1840, the mother and two daughters who used it carried on their small business, working from home until the late 1870s. When it was given to me by a member of one of the daughters' families, I had to promise never to disclose their name. The stigma which became attached to the workers of this beautiful embroidery when it was in its declining years seems incomprehensible. One dear old lady, who in her youth did some of the most delicate and intricate work I have ever seen, kept it hidden away; as it could not be found when she died, I suspect she may have destroyed it. She had no children of her own to wear the garments, so lovingly and patiently made. She was afraid that someone would find out she had been taught the craft in an orphanage – her home until she reached the age of twelve, after which she had to leave and make her living 'in service'.

The earliest wooden stamps, called 'blocks' by the flowerers, were hand carved (Fig 9). This in itself must have been a very skilled and exacting occupation. Later stamps (Fig 10) have patterns formed from strips of copper inserted in to the wood. Most of the stamps in my collection are engraved 'P. Wright, 12 Wellington Street, Glasgow', but I have been unable to find any documentation on this company.

Although it is known that a water-soluble dye was used to transfer the designs to the material, no one has ever been able to explain to me exactly how this was done. Someone in the past told me that the 'Flowerers' mixed water and

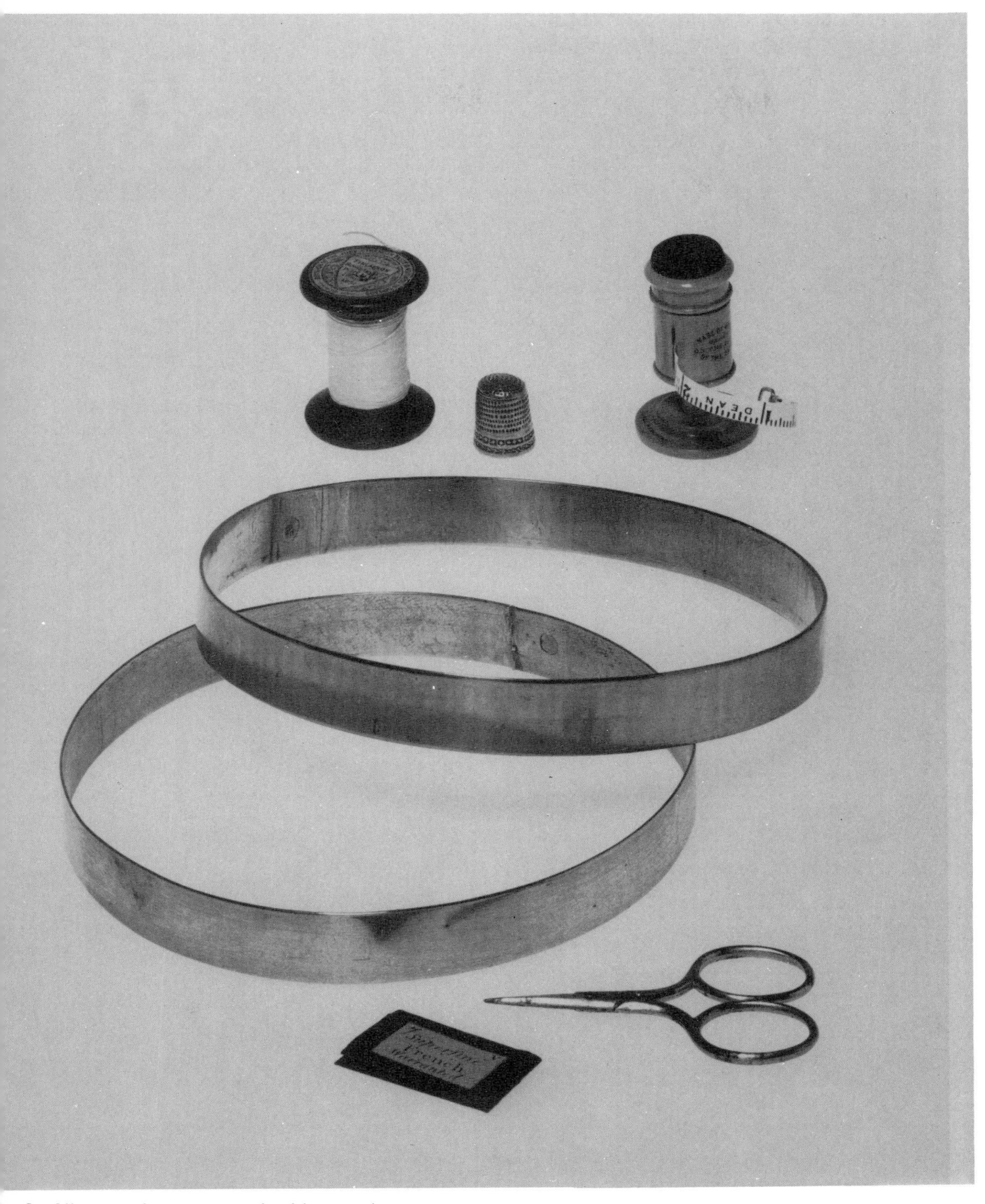

g 6 Nineteenth century embroidery tools
uthor's collection)

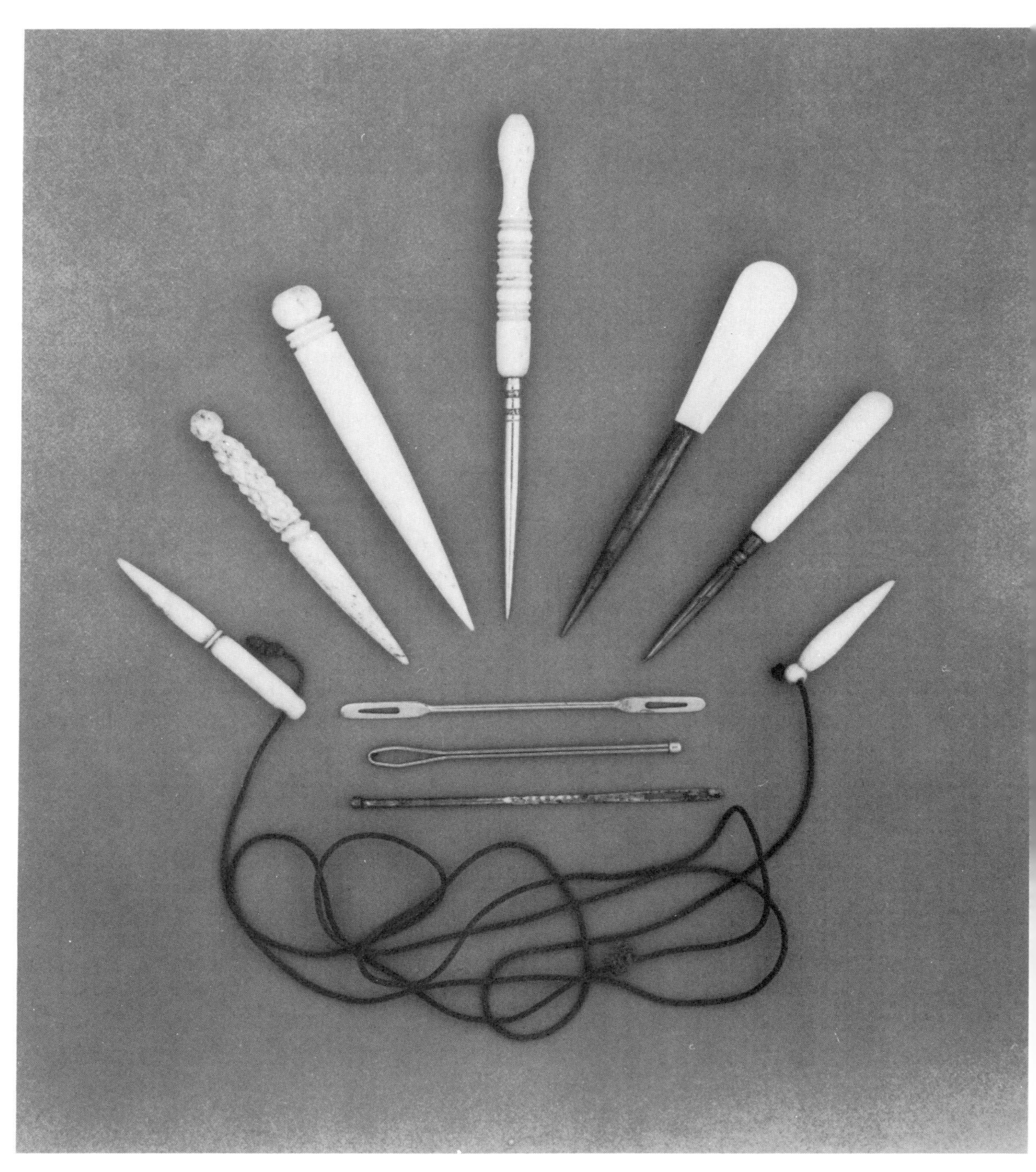

Fig 7 A selection of old stilettos and bodkins
(Author's collection)

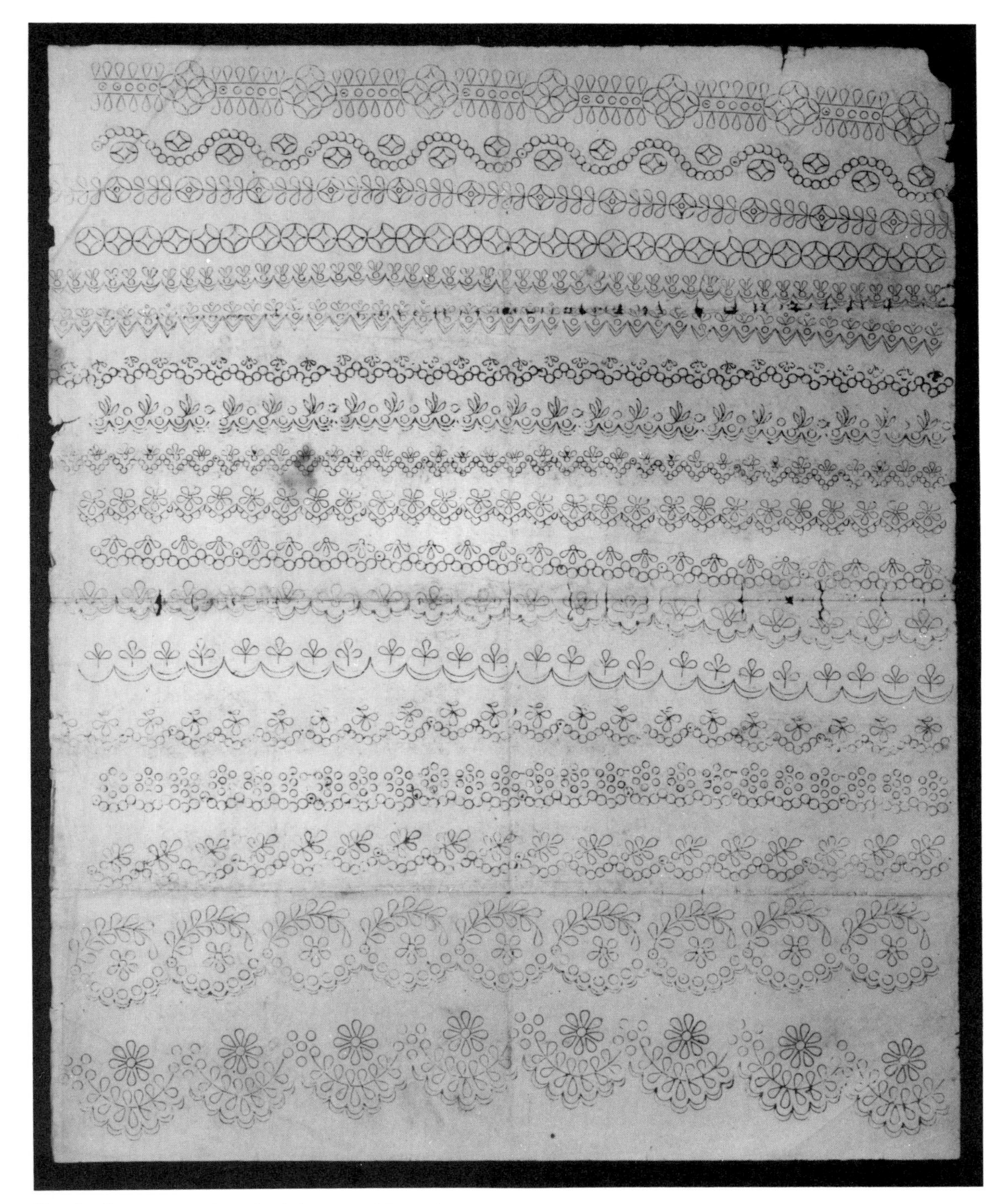

Fig 8 Paper sampler of edgings and insertions (Author's collection)

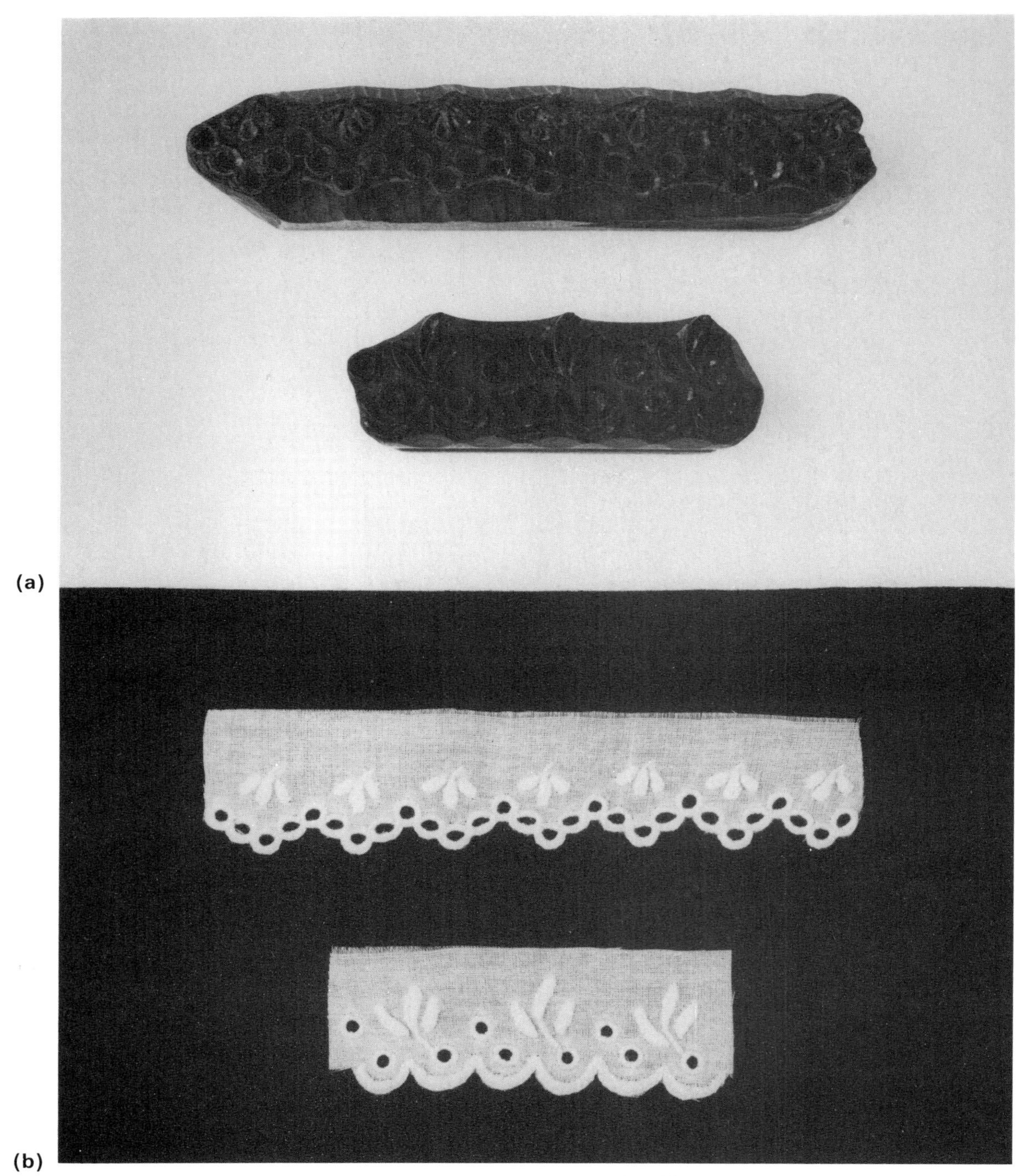

Fig 9 a) Two carved wooden stamps
b) Embroidered edgings worked by the author, using the stamps (Author's collection)

Right **Fig 10** Stamps with patterns formed from strips of copper inserted in to the wood, *c*. 1840–50 (Author's collection)

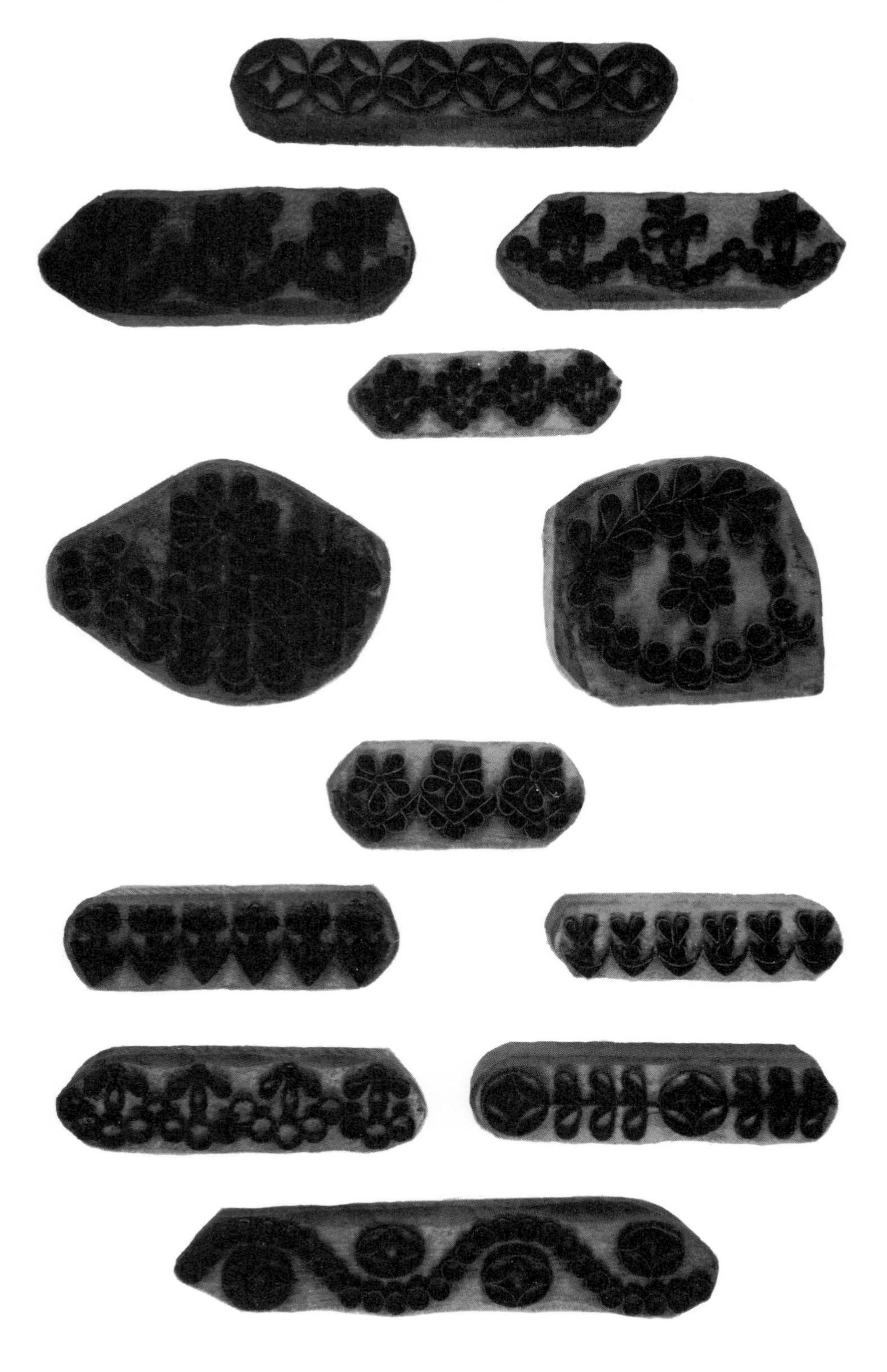

washing blue with ground sugar, which acted as a mordant. I therefore tried this, crushing the sugar with pestle and mortar before adding the water and washing blue. The result: bright blue icing, which set on the stamps and filled up all the holes in the designs. I then tried a solution of water and a lot of 'washing blue' which, even if it had been successful in transferring the design, would have been useless, as the colour was so strong it would not wash out. Next I made a much less colourful solution, again using washing blue, pinned my material out on a flat surface, and tried again. No pattern appeared; only a series of ugly blobs.

I laid the stamp down on a folded newspaper. When I removed it, there on the paper was a perfect impression of the design. I placed layers of blotting paper under the material, dipped the stamp in the solution and pressed it on the fabric. This worked reasonably well, giving quite a good impression, but still left water marks around the design. I then discovered that if the stamp is given a quick flick to remove any surplus solution after it has been dipped, a reasonable impression is obtained. Using a pad or roller soaked with the solution did not work, as the dye would not adhere to the metal designs. Still using a solution of washing blue and water, but using alum as a mordant, gave similar results.

At this point, I decided to take a closer look, with a magnifying glass, at a little green block about 2 cm by 1.5 cm which came in the box with the stamps. The lady who gave them to me referred to it as 'just a wee bit of chalk the Flowerers rubbed on the stamps'. On one side, in relief, it has a design of flowers, reminiscent of Ayrshire needlework, above which is an heraldic animal wearing a heavy collar and surmounted by a crown. Around the edge is a scalloped border. On the reverse is stamped 'CHROME GREEN', again with a pretty border of flowers and a design of trailing. The border on this side is in stem stitch. I discovered that this 'chalk' is really solid dye. If you wet it, apply it to the stamp, then press the stamp on your material, you get a perfect impression every time. I cannot confirm that this was the laborious method by which the designs were transferred, but it certainly works. Very few of these original Ayrshire needlework stamps remain. One old lady told me that her mother's method of transferring designs was to lay a fresh piece of material on

Fig 11 This stamp is called 'melon seed'. The stamps all had names, but these have been forgotten with the passage of time

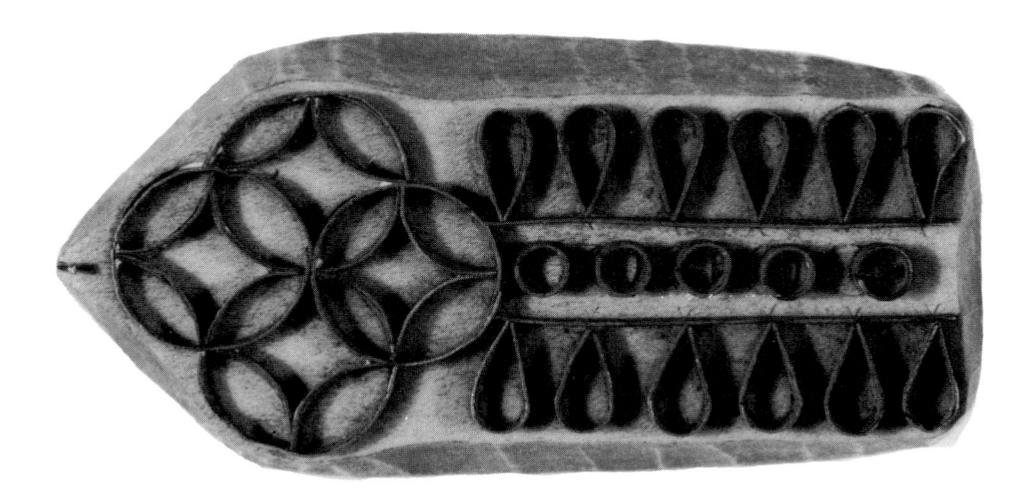

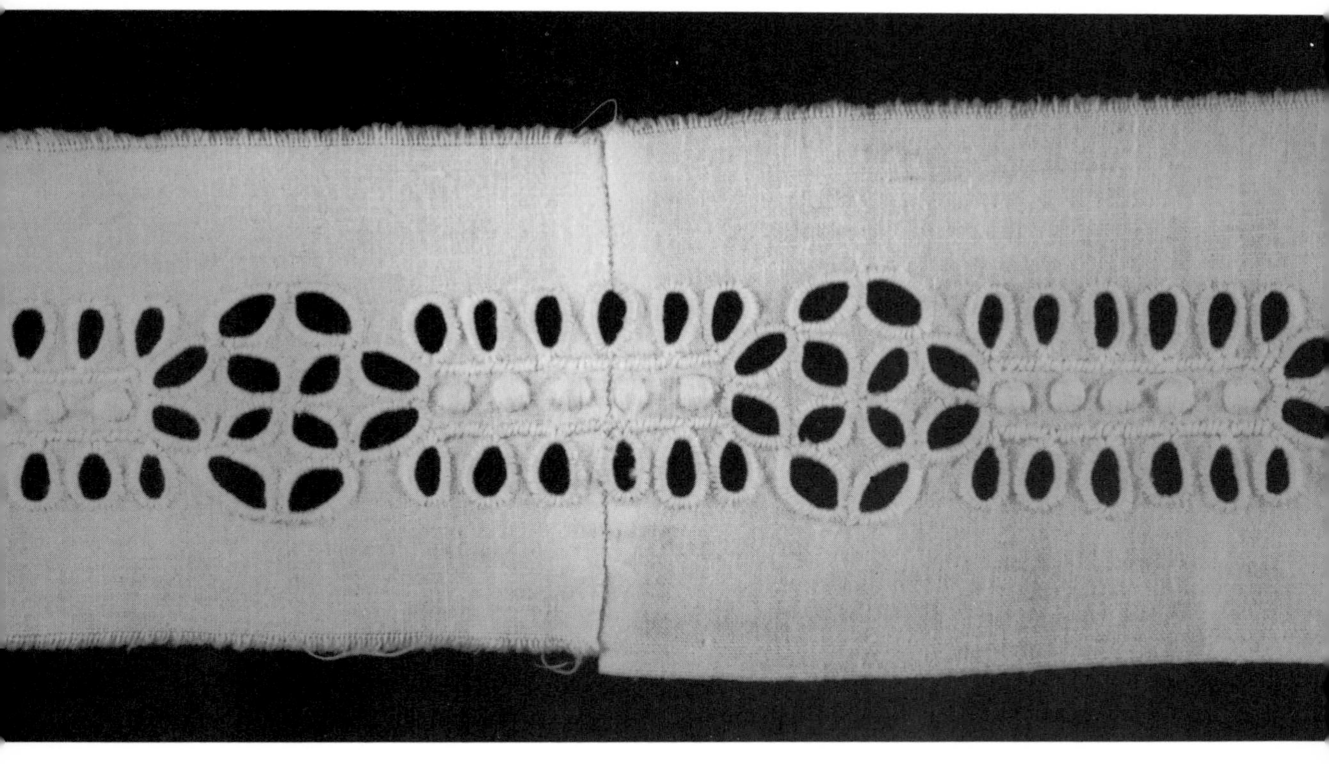

Fig 12 Piece worked in 1860 using the stamp in Fig 11 (Author's collection)

top of a completed piece of embroidery and make a rubbing with a pewter spoon.

The block in Fig 11 clearly shows a metal pin at the pointed end, which, when printed, fits on the small circle in the last eyelet so that the pattern can easily be run off in a continuous line. All the blocks with copper inserted designs have these 'lining-up pins'.

Fig 12 shows a piece made in 1860–70, using the block in Fig 11. Note how the material has been joined and the embroidery worked over the join. The material is of poor quality and very coarse – not at all in keeping with the fine lawn still in common use during this period. The piece is about three metres long and, according to the friend who gave it to me, was made by her Grandmother to be inserted into a lady's underskirt.

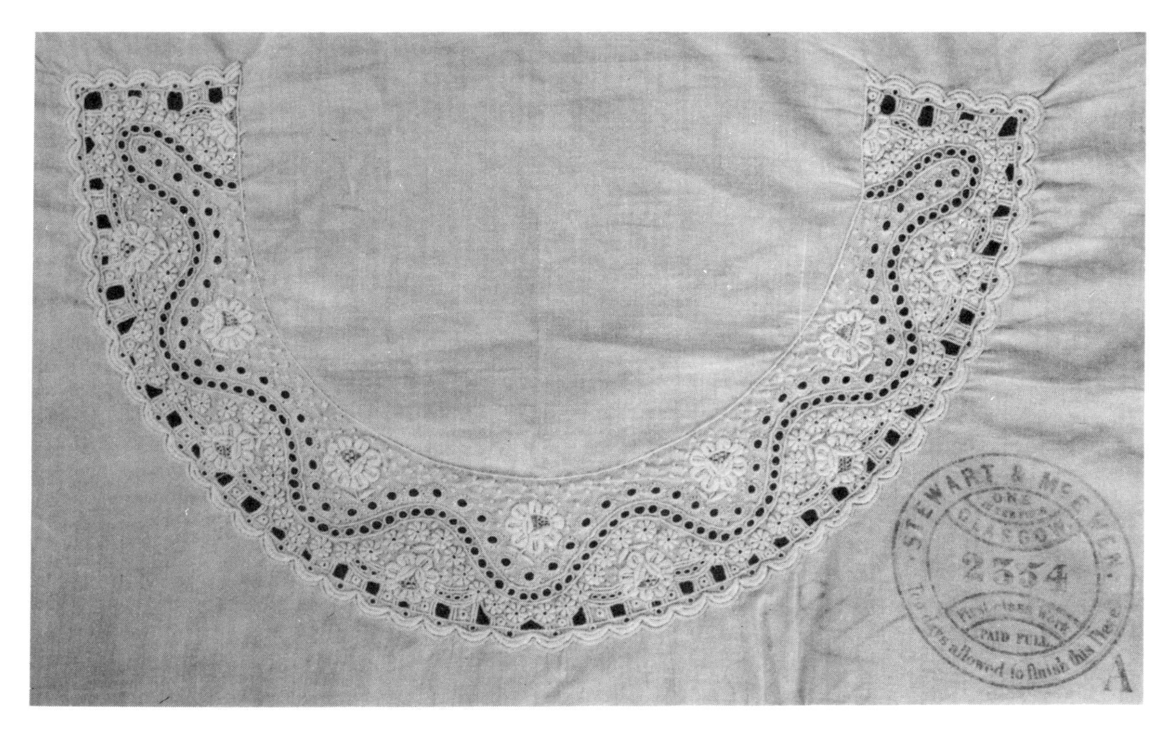

Fig 13 An embroidered collar still uncut from the foundation material (Glasgow Museums and Art Galleries, reproduced by permission)

Fig 13 is a collar embroidered and ready to be returned to the warehouse of Stewart & McEwen, Glasgow, to be laundered, cut from the foundation material, packaged and sent out to the retail trade to be sold. When the flowerer first received the stamped material, the requisite amount of thread to work the piece would be included with it. The stamp shows clearly that ten days were allowed to finish the piece. The completed embroidery was considered to be first-class work, and paid for in full. It also shows that there was only one design stamped on this particular piece of foundation material. The 'Flowering' agents were very strict, and meticulous in their methods of distribution and collection.

Fig 14 Bottom of front panel on a robe showing the solid embroidery worked, but the needlelace fillings still undone (Glasgow Museum and Art Galleries, reproduced by permission)

Fig 14 shows that the solid embroidery was worked first by the less skilled embroideresses, who left the open-work spaces – blank areas surrounded by satin or outline stitch – undone. This more technically difficult stage in the embroidery was worked by the most experienced embroideresses, who specialised in needlelace stitches and received a higher rate of pay. The repair shows that this robe has been worn, although the embroidery has not been completed.

Fig 15 A bassinet cover made for the Great Exhibition in 1851 (Glasgow Museums and Art Galleries, reproduced by permission)

Fig 16 Detail of bassinet cover (Glasgow Museums and Art Galleries, reproduced by permission)

Fig 17 Sampler bonnet of needlepoint fillings. Tucks in Ayrshire needlework bonnets were made not for decoration but to contain the tapes which moulded it to the shape of the child's head (see Fig 4) (Author's collection)

Fig 15 is a bassinet cover, believed to have been made for the 1851 Exhibition, which was sponsored by the Royal Society of Arts and staged in the Crystal Palace, Hyde Park, London. It may also have been Exhibit 27 at:

THE:GLASGOW:SCHOOL:OF:ART.
EXHIBITION:OF:ANCIENT:&:
MODERN:EMBROIDERY:&:
NEEDLECRAFT:1916.
French linen hand spun cambric, rose, thistle, and shamrock design. Shows 3 or 4 stitches; cannot be done to-day. Coral, drawn thread, padded work. A clever and beautifully constructed design, incorporating all the national emblems – daffodil, rose, shamrock and thistle. The delicate needle-made lace edging is a most intricate piece of work.

Fig 18 Detail of bonnet crown

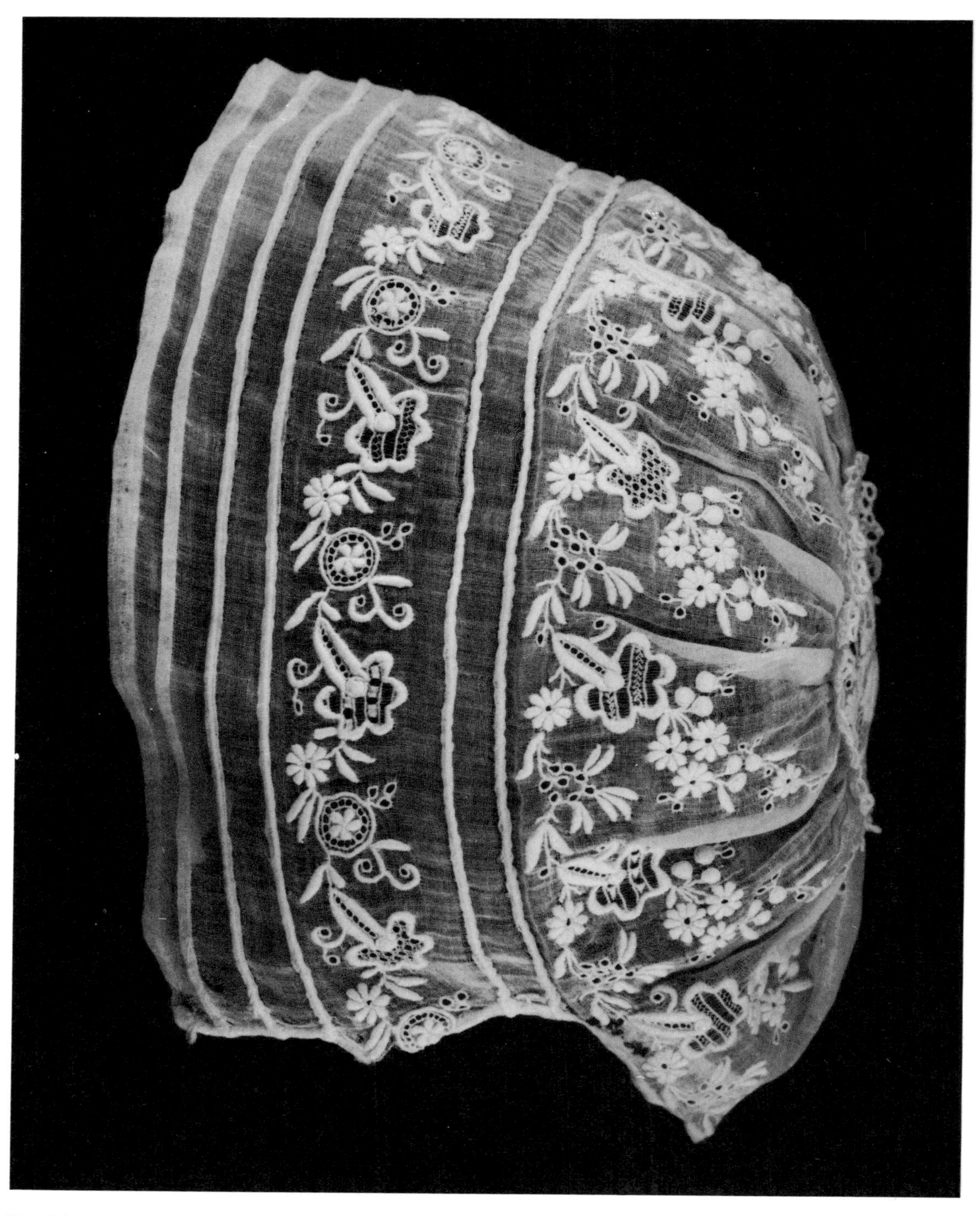

Fig 19 A delightful little bonnet, *c.* 1820, worked on muslin which is almost transparent (Glasgow Museums and Art Galleries, reproduced by permission)

Fig 20 Detail of crown of Fig 19

Fig 16 shows a detail of the bassinet cover in Fig 15, showing the beautifully constructed design combining all the national symbols – the daffodil, rose, shamrock and thistle. The bonnet in Fig 17 is like a little sampler of needlepoint fillings, 57 in all, no two of which are exactly alike. In the early part of the ninteenth century baby bonnets were tied on top of the head to prevent choking. The string used to secure this one can only just be seen at the top. The crown shown in Fig 18, is typical of the period, containing a lot of openwork, which allowed the baby's head to perspire freely.

A bonnet *c.* 1820, worked on very fine muslin or cambric, is shown in Fig 19. The gentians in the design are worked in a variety of drawn fabric and drawn thread stitches. Fig 20 shows a detail.

Fig 21 A very elaborate christening robe (Glasgow Museums and Art Galleries, reproduced by permission)

Fig 22 Detail of front panel on the robe in Fig 21 (Glasgow Museums and Art Galleries, reproduced by permission)

The sleeves of the very elaborate robe in Fig 21 are simply layers of frills, but the skirt is very long – 109 cm (43 in) – and voluminous. The detail of the front panel (Fig 22) shows a considerable selection of flowers: daisies with delicate needlepoint centres, lilacs, or perhaps a floral treatment of bunches of grapes; tulips in many forms; wind grasses and an attractive treatment of the gentian, which was a very popular flower with the 'Flowerers'. A line of laddering has been worked beside the stitching line, where the 'wings' – the name used by the Flowerers for the flat embroidered frills – are attached to the skirt.

In the *Dictionary of English Costume* 900–1900, by C. Willet Cunnington, these frills are referred to as 'Robin' or 'Robings':

> Broad flat trimmings decorating a gown round the neck and down the front of the bodice, and sometimes continued down the borders of an open overskirt to the hem.

On the bodice very little of the ground material can be seen, so concentrated is the embroidery (Fig 23). Note how well each individual section of robe matches the other pieces: even the waistband is a simplified version of the edging to the neckline, which is very dainty and intricate. I have seen the same edging used on other robes, so it must have been a standard design.

Fig 23 Detail of bodice on the robe in Fig 21 (Glasgow Museums and Art Galleries, reproduced by permission)

Fig 24 A unique robe embroidered with nursery rhyme characters (Glasgow Museums and Art Galleries, reproduced by permission)

Fig 25 Detail of Fig 24: Jack and Jill, with Jill rubbing Jack's broken crown

Fig 24 is an early (probably 1820) and most unusual robe, worked on an extremely sheer muslin and showing nursery rhymes in a great variety of stitches and appliqué. Near the top of the panel is a sheep worked in drawn thread. Fig 25 shows Jack and Jill, with Jill rubbing Jack's broken crown (Detail of Fig 24). Worked right across the panel is 'Mary, Mary quite contrary, how does your garden grow?' (Fig 26). The detail clearly shows how a much heavier lawn has been applied very effectively to the leaves and flowers to emphasize the design and speed of the work.

This robe is the only one on which I have seen appliqué used, so it leads me to believe that this technique was unusual.

The bottom third of the front panel (Fig 27) is most delicately worked with a considerable number of drawn thread and drawn fabric fillings, interspersed with appliqué, solid embroidery and eyelets, giving the effect of lace. Because such sheer material is no longer available, it would be impossible to reproduce embroidery of this standard. The finest lawn produced today is of a weight similar to that used here for the appliqué. The open weave of the material gives a light airiness to the openwork fillings in this garment.

Top right **Fig 26** Detail of Fig 24: Mary, Mary, quite contrary

Bottom right **Fig 27** Bottom of the front panel of Fig 24 showing appliqué, drawn thread and drawn fabric stitches

Fig 28 The bodice of a pre-1830 robe (Glasgow Museums and Art Galleries, reproduced by permission)

Fig 28 shows a robe which probably dates from before 1830, when it became fashionable to allow the triangular tip of the bodice to extend below the waist. It has been altered by adding sleeves in a material of inferior quality under the original cap sleeves, to lengthen them. This may have been done at the beginning of the twentieth century, when longer sleeves became fashionable. At about this time many dresses had new bodices of machine-made embroidery and long sleeves added to them, while in others the original sleeves were removed, replaced by long ones, and the cap sleeves returned at the wrists to become cuffs. This gave the robe the appearance of being complete and, to the untrained eye, quite authentic. Another reason for replacing bodices may have been that they required harder rubbing in the wash to remove food stains, which meant that they fell apart while the skirt remained intact. I have seen many robes with new bodices and feel this proves that these robes were everyday wear during the heyday of the 'Flowering'. The cap, or cape, sleeve is much more practical than a fitted one, as it fits either a small or large baby. There is no restriction on the arm. The neck has a very open buttonholed square eyelet edging.

The embroidery on the front panel (Fig 29) shows very firm, bold outlines to the design and unusual fillings in the leaves. Some of these have laddering separated by bars of satin stitch, while others have delicate drawn thread fillings surrounded by a heavy border of seeding. Again there are gentian and lilac type flowers, and

Fig 29 Detail of skirt from Fig 28 (Glasgow Museums and Art Galleries, reproduced by permission)

Fig 30 Bottom of the front panel on a robe with the unusual combination of shadow work and Ayrshire needlework (Glasgow Museums and Art Galleries, reproduced by permission)

quite large areas of a detached buttonhole stitch filling. Fillings in the large eyelet holes are just simple 'spider webs', but very effective. The eyelet edging at the bottom of the panel has a second row of buttonhole stitch which, apart from adding strength, looks most attractive.

The bottom section on the front panel of a robe (Fig 30) shows shadow work used very effectively on the petals of the larger flowers. This is the only robe on which I have seen shadow work done, which leads me to conclude that this technique was rarely used. I have experimented with this technique and found that even the finest cotton lawn now available is not sufficiently transparent to be effective. The square eyelets worked at random on a drawn

Fig 31 Detail of darned net fillings (by kind permission of Margaret H. Swain)

Fig 32 Another aspect of nature in Ayrshire needlework: a robe with peacocks and butterflies (Glasgow Museums and Art Galleries, reproduced by permission)

thread background produce a very pretty filling.

A detail from a baby robe (Fig 31) showing embroidered net used in place of needle made lace fillings. Using darned net may have been a short cut to speed up the work, or perhaps no embroideress capable of doing the needlelace stitches was available. This could also be borne out by the very simple spider web fillings in the eyelets.

A robe showing another aspect of nature in Ayrshire Needlework is seen in Fig 32. The wings of the butterflies alighting on the flowers, in the upper motifs, and the bodies and necks of the birds have beautifully worked needlepoint fillings. The peacock being the symbol of immortality may have been the inspiration behind the use of this motif.

Fig 33 Fichu (Glasgow Museums and Art Galleries, reproduced by permission)

Below **Fig 34** A child's embroidered bodice (Collection of Kyle and Carrick District Library and Museum Services)

Fig 35 An updated robe (Author's collection)

A fichu, made for Wilson & Sutherland, 37 Cathedral Street, Glasgow is in Fig 33. These broad collars became very fashionable during the 1850s, and were worn over the shoulders like a cape. The ends were crossed or tied on the bosom. Because of the translucency of the material, the embroidery was shown off to perfection, when it was worn over a dark dress.

Although there is no documentation on this garment (Fig 34), it is known to have belonged to a Catholic family, and may have had a religious connection. It would fit an 8 to 10 year old child, so perhaps it was lovingly homemade, or commissioned for a First Communion. It is fastened with buttons on the shoulders, and when worn over a simple dark dress the embroidery would be shown off to considerable advantage. I expect the little girl who owned it wore it with pride, but I am certain it would have little appeal for the modern child.

By the beginning of the twentieth century, it became fashionable to have lace insertions on christening robes. Fig 35 shows a very ingenious conversion. Imagine the insertions and lace removed from the bottom edge, and you have an original Ayrshire needlework robe. This updated robe has been destroyed as far as the connoisseur is concerned, but it is for the eye of the beholder to judge whether the conversion is an improvement or not. I have seen several robes which have been updated in this manner. The owners must have been very fashion-conscious.

By this time, new christening robes were no longer made of handmade Ayrshire needlework, but rather of machine-made imitation. The traditional shape of the peaked bodice and triangular skirt panel had disappeared. In their place was a very full straight skirt with horizontal bands of machine-made insertion. The 'wings', or broad flat frills, were still retained, but would extend from the hem right up over the shoulders. Small puff sleeves replaced the cap or cape sleeves. The material between the insertions was hand-embroidered with feather stitching, which was also used on the neckline, waistband and cuffs to give the garment a hand-made appearance. The central medallion near the bottom of the panel on Fig 35 is of style which frequently appears on robes. The grid of beading, or back stitch with single eyelets, is very effective and would have been quick and easy to work. It has no needlepoint fillings and may have been made at the time of the demise of the craft as a commercial enterprise.

I have seen many little Ayrshire needlework bonnets transformed by the simple addition of layer upon layer of lace to frame the face. Satin ribbons, so out of harmony with the cotton lawn, were attached to secure the bonnet under the chin with a bow. Recently, I removed the satin ribbons and over a metre of machine-made lace from a bonnet, to find that the lace had obscured a beautifully embroidered little Ayrshire needlepoint baby's cap, still complete with the original string ties on top of the head. The owner was delighted to have her treasured little bonnet restored to its original state.

Ayrshire needlework was also used on children's and ladies' dresses, underwear, bonnets, collars and handkerchiefs. The design most commonly used on older children's clothing was from the stamp called 'Melon Seed' (Fig 11). Handkerchiefs, made by schoolgirls and called 'wedding handkerchiefs', were quite large for a lady's handkerchief, usually about 35 cm square. When a child completed her embroidery, it was carefully wrapped and stored in her dower chest until her wedding day. These handkerchiefs always have the name of the embroideress written on them with indelible ink. This leads me to believe that the teacher may have been working from one pattern, and the names were added as a means of identification.

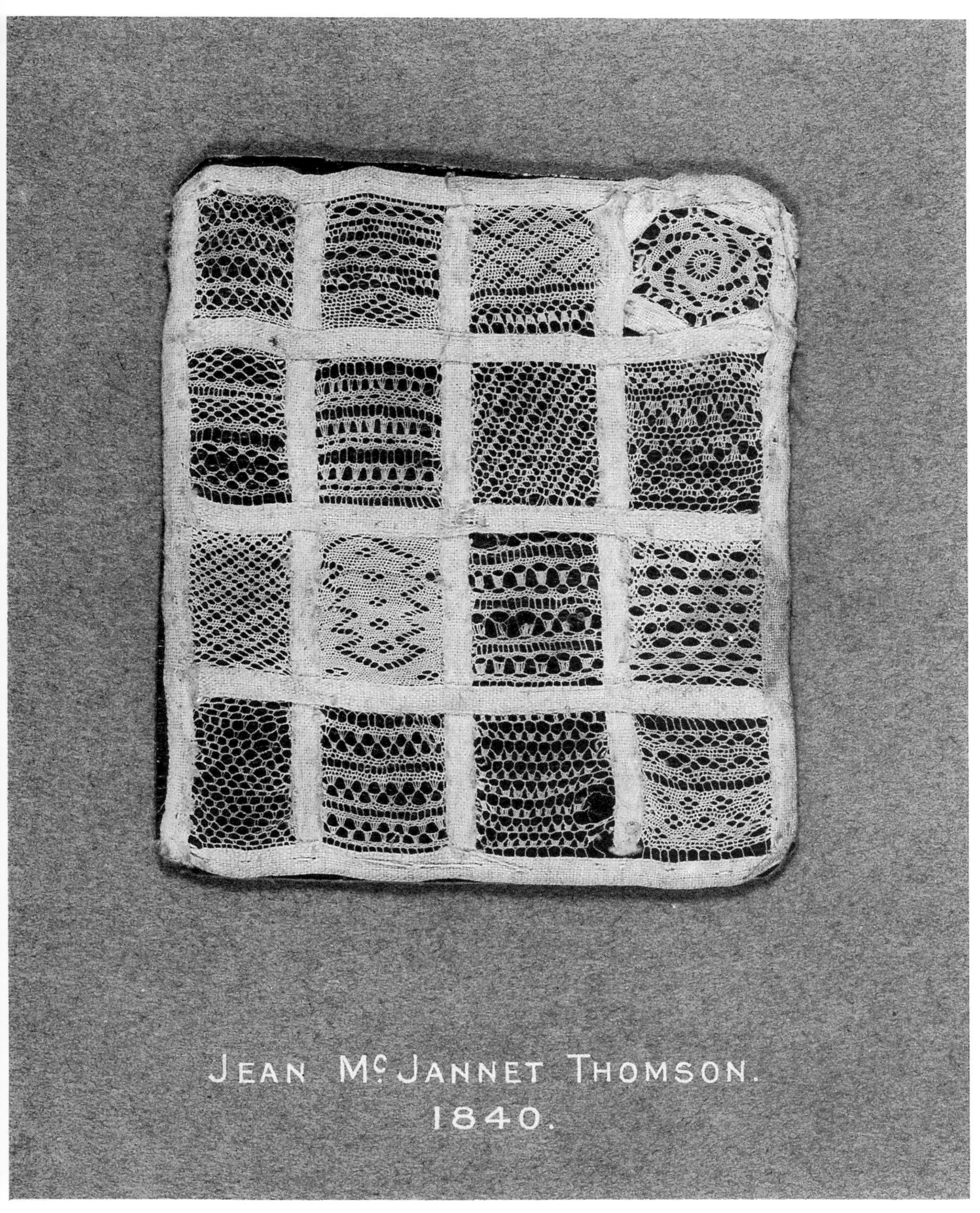

Fig 36 Sampler of needlelace stitches worked by Jean McJanet Thomson in 1840 (Author's collection)

9 A nineteenth-century model washday

The day before the washing the white clothes ought to be soaked in soap, melted in hot water, and a little washing soda. This loosens the grease and saves rubbing, which wears out the material very much.

Chloride of lime will remove all marks and stains, but requires to be very carefully used, as it is of an excessively burning nature, and the stain may be replaced by a hole. There is little danger, however, if the part is wet, and the chloride of lime diluted a little.

Stains of mildew are difficult to remove. Rub with soap, wet well, and expose to the sun and the air for several days, always keeping the stains wet and soaped. A little fine chalk rubbed over the place while wet and in the air sometimes removes the stains, but chloride of lime, applied in the manner previously described, is the easiest way.

Begin work early on washing day. The best part of the day is in the forenoon, and an hour gained in the morning is worth two later in the day.

The first thing to do is to light the boiler fire.

Wash out the soaked clothes carefully, removing all stains. The soaking will have rendered hard rubbing almost unnecessary. Put them into another tub with warm water, and wash again. Then have a tub with plenty of cold water in it; drop them into this, and let them lie for a short time.

Fill up the boiler with cold water. Wring the clothes roughly out of the cold water, and put them in the boiler; cover with the lid, and let them boil gently for about ten to fifteen minutes. The rinsing in cold water before they are boiled has the great advantage of removing all the dirty water from the clothes, otherwise it gets boiled into them, and injures the colour.

When boiled enough, take them out of the boiler. Now pour some cold water on the boiled clothes, wash them out, and rinse twice. The water they are rinsed in first had better be hot, as it extracts the soap much better than cold water ever will. Let them be well wrung out of the last rinsing. They must now be blued, that is, put in water tinged with blue.

Put in a tub a small quantity of water, and tinge it well with blue. Never allow clothes to lie in blue water, or more than one in at a time; but just dip once or twice, and wring out.

In the country, or wherever possible, after boiling, let the clothes be spread out on the grass to bleach. The sun and air have a magical effect in whitening, and they impart to it a sweetness and perfume which dwellers in the town can only envy.

After bleaching, rinse and blue as described above.

Plenty of clear water, the sun and air, are the cheapest of all devices for making cottons white and sweet, combined, of course, with the use of an active pair of hands.

Fine muslins must not be rubbed, but squeezed between the hands in melted soap and warm water until they are clean. When to be boiled, they should be put in a little bag or bundle by themselves, to prevent them from getting torn, and afterwards rinsed in the usual way. They do not require to be hung up to dry. They are just folded, rolled up in a clean towel, clapped, and put aside to be starched.

Cold water starch

Have some white soap cut down thinly, and melt it with a little hot water. [I cannot understand why soap was added to the starch when so much trouble had been taken to remove it before this stage was reached.] Have powdered borax, or lump borax powdered down.

The proportions given below are for Coleman's starch, but any good starch suits, and the proportions can easily be ascertained by a single trial.

Put in a basin 3 small tablespoonfuls of starch, and wet it to a paste with a large teacupful of cold water.

Put into a cup a teaspoonful of the melted white soap, and a teaspoonful of the borax, and dissolve them in half a teacupful of boiling water. Pour this now into the basin with the starch, and mix them well together till a nice froth gathers on the top.

This starch is most suitable for collars, cuffs, etc., but does very well for muslin or cotton if diluted with cold water.

Boiled water starch

This is much the best and nicest starch for muslins, and all fine fabrics.

Ingredients required: – Starch, composite candle, spermaceti, turpentine, boiling water.

Warm a basin well with boiling water, and pour it out again.

Put into the basin 4 tablespoonfuls of starch, and rub it down to a rather thick paste with warm water; add an inch of a small-sized composite candle, a bit of spermaceti, size of a small bean, and 4 drops of turpentine. Pour boiling water into the basin slowly, stirring very vigorously till the starch is cooked sufficiently, which is known by its becoming transparent. It ought to be a good thickness, not in the least watery. Use the starch at once, and very hot, as it quickly becomes thick, and is not easily used.

Extracts from *Mrs Black's Household Cookery and Laundry Work*, published by Wm Collins, Sons & Co., Limited, London and Glasgow.

10 Projects worked by the author

Fig 37 Crown for a baby's bonnet

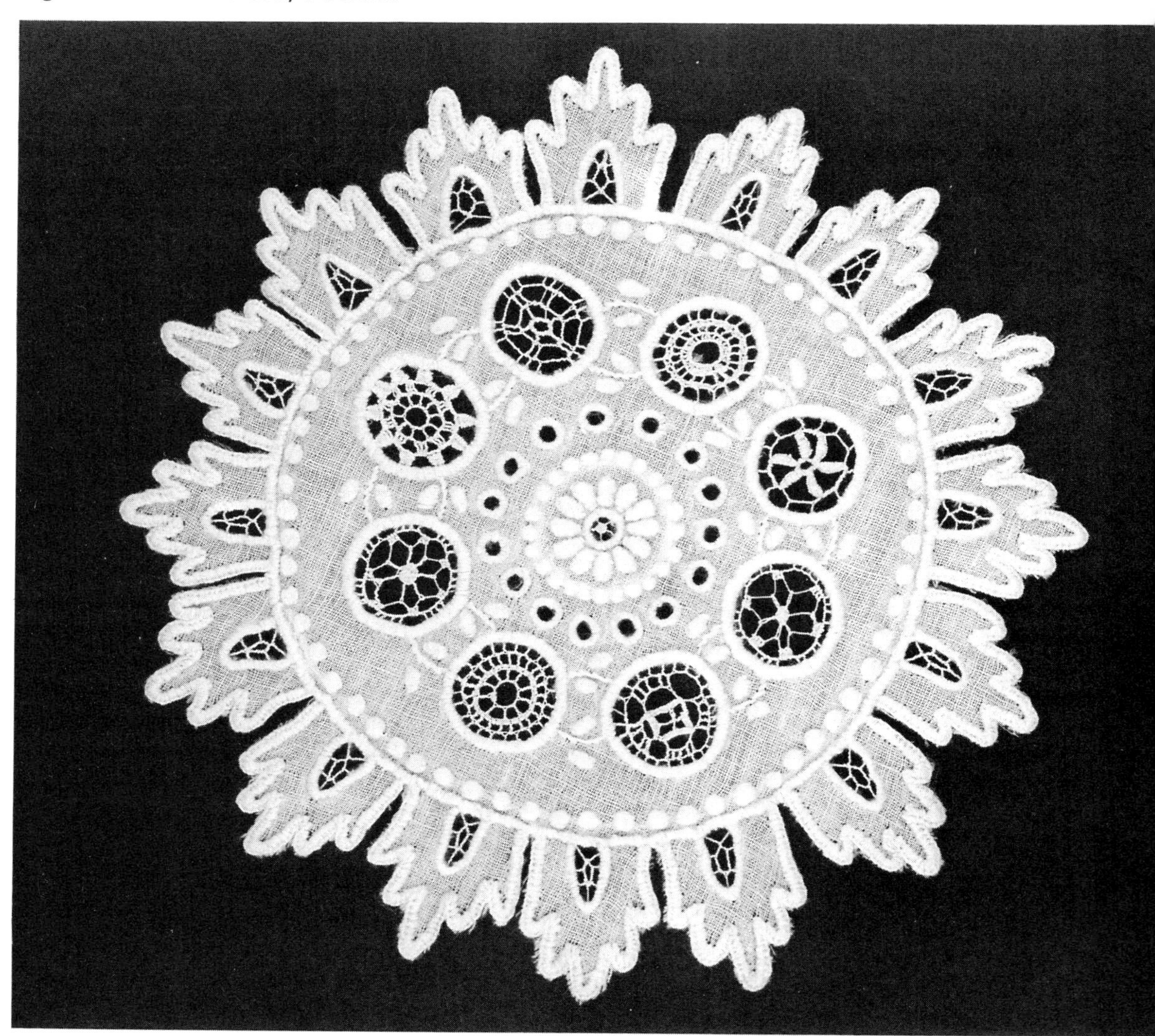

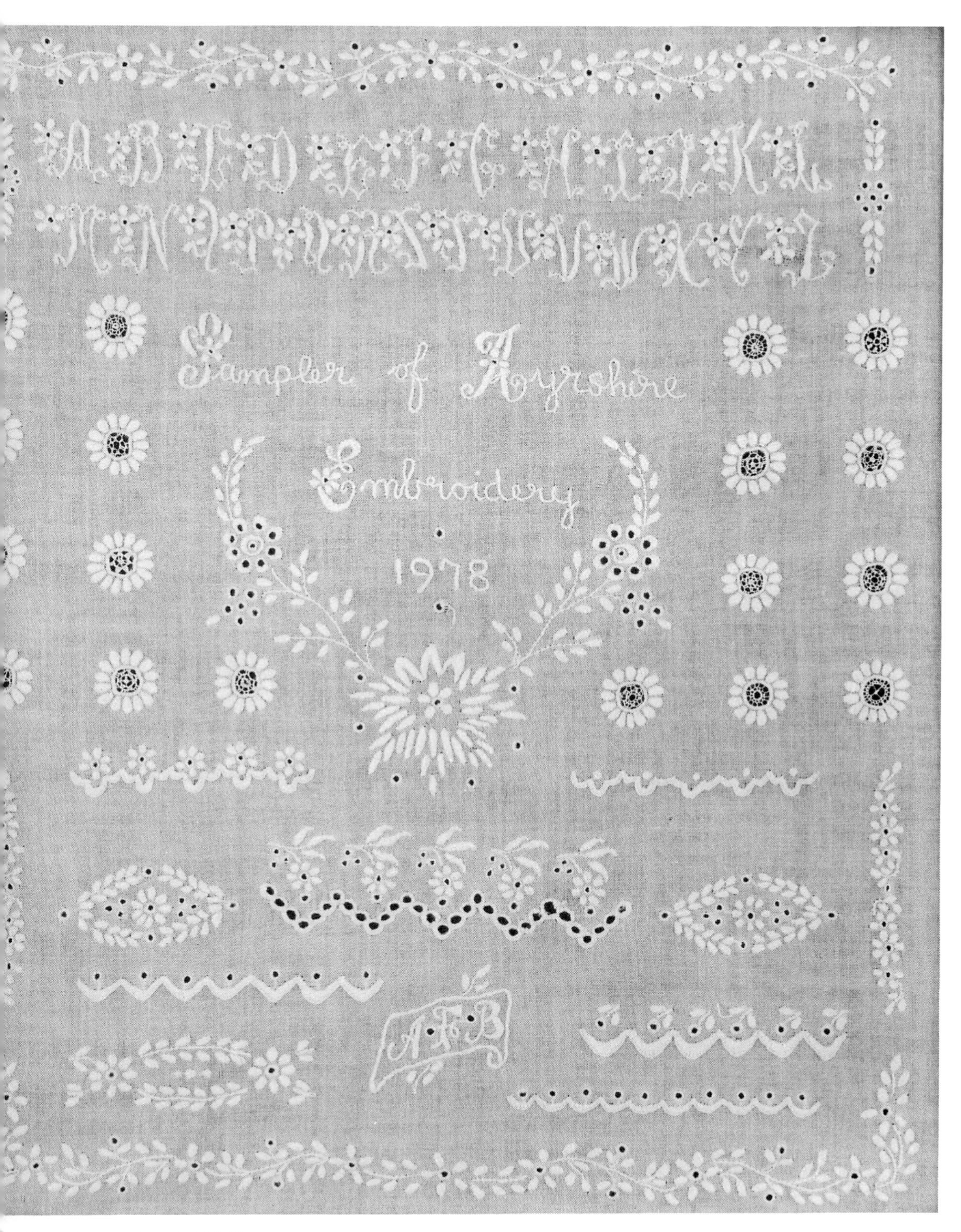

Sampler worked in 1978

1. Crown for a baby's bonnet, worked from my own design (Fig 37). This was one of my earliest experiments in working needlepoint filling stitches. The solid embroidery was done with a No. 60 cotton thread and the fillings with an old unnumbered thread, possibly a No. 120. This old thread was firmer and held its shape much better than any of the modern threads I have worked with since.
2. In this sampler (Fig 38) I succumbed to the twentieth-century fashion of calling the technique Ayrshire embroidery. There are eighteen different needlepoint fillings, each about 7 mm in diameter, and worked with a No. 120 thread. The solid embroidery is worked with a No. 60 cotton sewing thread, which has had the twist taken out by the method described in the chapter *Materials, tools and hints*. This treatment gives the threads the appearance of the soft cotton used by the 'Flowerers', and the stitches blend beautifully into each other. A selection of small designs and edgings are also used. The alphabet is in keeping with the 'Flowering' style, and could be used for personalising small articles such as handkerchiefs. This is not a working sampler which I recommend that all who work this technique should use, but rather a piece designed to be framed and hung. It was worked on a piece of architect's linen, with the design bleached out.

Fig 39 Glasgow robe (Glasgow Museums and Art Galleries, reproduced by permission)

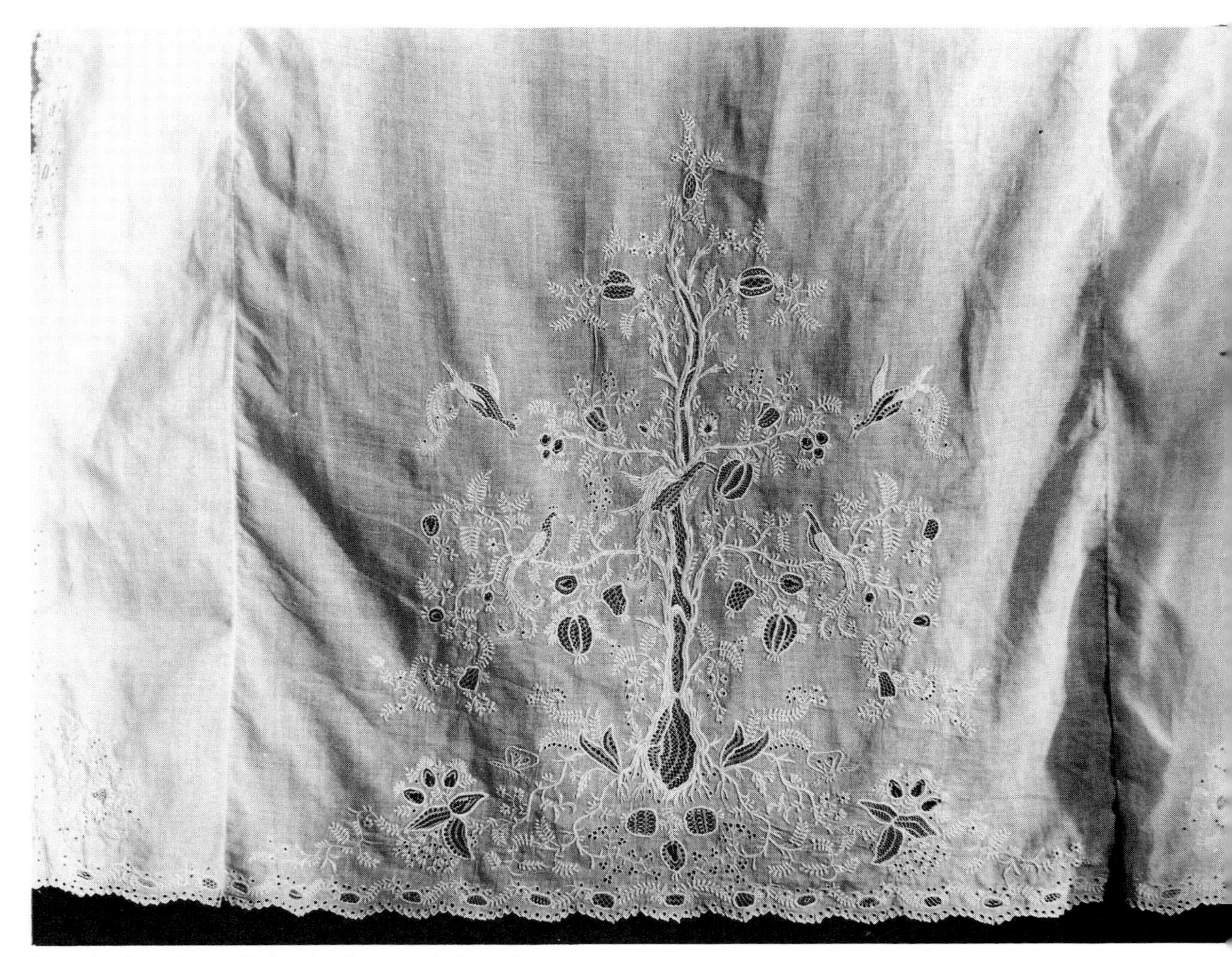

Fig 40 Gawthorpe Hall robe (by permission of the Trustees of the Rachel Kay Shuttleworth Collections)

3. In 1985 I found two robes, one (Fig 39) in the Glasgow Museums and Art Galleries collection, and the other (Fig 40) at Gawthorpe Hall, with the same design. After studying the robes and noting the differences in the completed embroideries, I set about working my own interpretation. I assume that these two old robes were not worked by the same embroideress, and feel that this is substantiated by the completely different approach to the working of open spaces in the birds and the tree trunk. The fillings used on the Gawthorpe Hall robe (Fig 41) are superior and technically much more difficult to work than those on the Glasgow Museums and Art Galleries robe (Fig 42). In Fig 40 a variety of fine needlelace fillings have been introduced into the border along the bottom edge, whereas in Fig 39 only simple eyelets have been worked. In this robe, however, a very dainty border is taken right up the sewing line where the 'wing' (flat frill) is attached to the skirt. The robe in Fig 39 has been cut down to make a short dress.

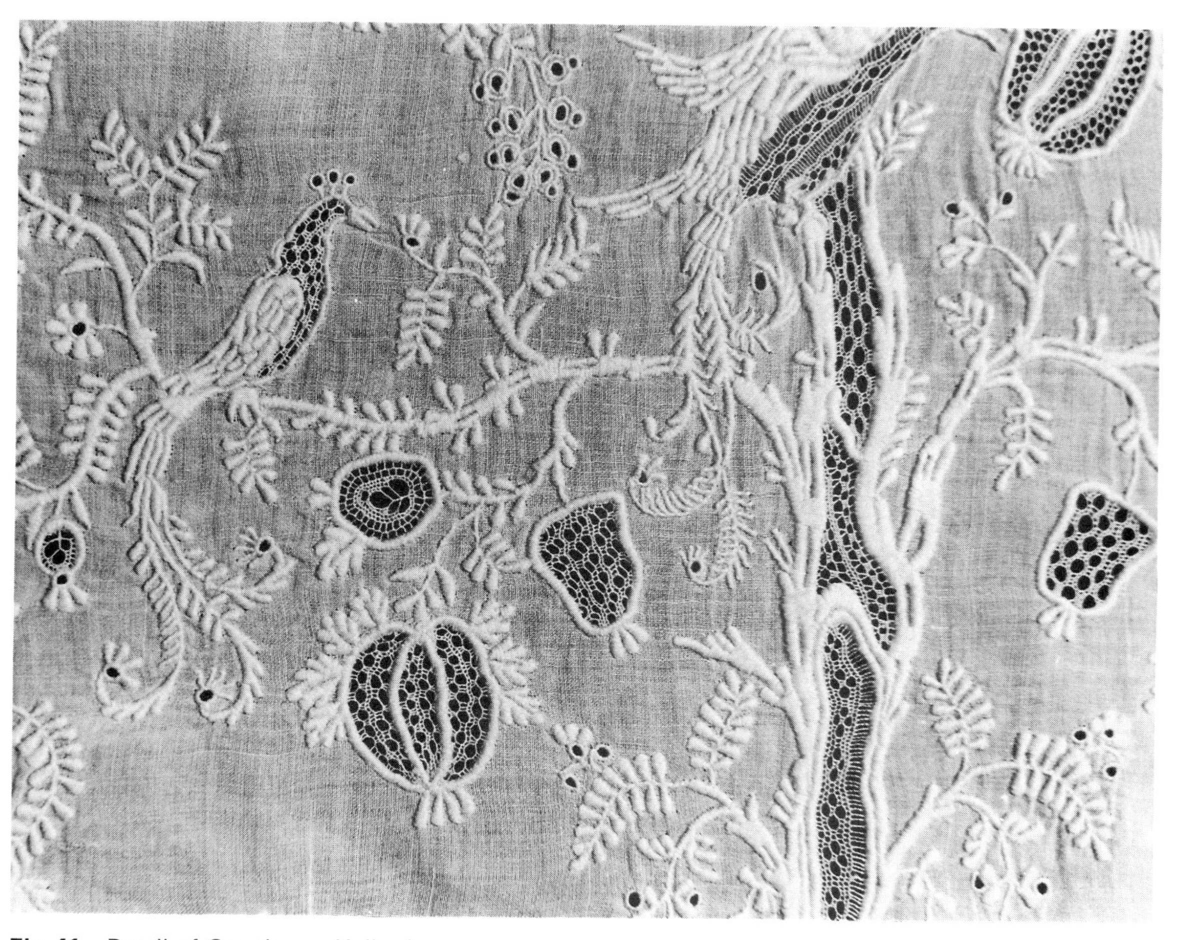

Fig 41 Detail of Gawthorpe Hall robe

Fig 42 Detail of robe in Fig 39

Fig 43 Tree of Life panel. Author's interpretation of the design in Figs 39 and 40, worked in 1986

Fig 44 Detail from Fig 43

Fig 45 Part of a beautiful robe with a central medallion (Mrs Margaret Service)

My interpretation of the two designs, worked to be framed and hung, is shown in Fig 43. The detail (Fig 44) shows clearly how, although I have only used variations of four-sided stitch, at first glance the impression of quite different openwork fillings is given. I left a single vertical thread between the four-sided stitches on the trunk; on some of the fruits there is a single vertical and horizontal thread, and on the others a simple four-sided stitch. The pomegranate was a favourite motif, perhaps because it was the symbol of plenty and fertility.

I needed a magnifying glass to count the threads of the fine lawn. I will never comprehend how the 'Flowerers' managed to work these intricate stitches by the light of a candle, without any mechanical aids.

4. The robe in Fig 45, which belongs to a friend, is the most beautiful I have ever seen. The perfection of the embroidery and the technical skill of the embroideress are beyond compare. I can only hazard a guess at the number of patient hours it took to complete. When I borrowed it, my intention was to reproduce the whole garment, but after spending over 200 hours working a copy of the medallion near the bottom of the skirt panel, I decided to abandon my original plan and frame up the piece I had completed.

Fig 46 Detail of medallion from Fig 45

Fig 47 An oval sampler worked by the author

5. Oval sampler. The oval medallion is actually a sampler of all the stitches (except four-sided) and drawn thread fillings used in Ayrshire needlework. For the embroidery I used the finest cotton lawn available now, but it is not nearly as fine as that used in the robe (Fig 45). This can be observed by comparing the weight of the foundation material in the detail of the robe (Fig 45), and the detail of my embroidery (Fig 48).

Fig 48 Detail from Fig 47

Fig 49 Bodice of a robe worked by author *Below* **Fig 50** Skirt from Fig 49

Fig 51 Bonnet to match robe in Fig 49

6. Designing and embroidering the christening set of matching robe (Figs 49,50), bonnet (Fig 51) and underskirt took me almost two years. I took the idea for the embroidery on the skirt panel from a family heirloom. It is the only design I have seen which incorporates an urn. Of the original robe, only the skirt remains: the bodice has been replaced by one with long sleeves which is machine-made, and has no embroidery. I had to design a completely new bodice, introducing motifs from the skirt panel to give continuity to the overall design.

To work out the complicated construction of the bodice I made a robe for a doll (Fig 52), using it as a sampler for the design and the stitches. The christening robe and bonnet were made from old material which had been

Fig 52 Dressed doll

handed in to a charity shop. The tiny linen buttons and tape used to secure it came from an antique work box and may be well over a hundred years old. It took me almost 1000 metres of No. 60 sewing cotton to complete the embroidery.

11 Materials, tools, stitches and hints

Ayrshire needlework can be very tiring for the eyes and I would suggest that anyone new to the technique only sew for very short periods until her eyes have become accustomed to working with white thread on white material. I always encourage my students to practise using white on white for a few weeks before attending my classes.

Some of the Flowerers dipped their thread, on the reel, in a mild solution of washing blue. The contrast when working with the slightly tinted thread made a considerable difference to the eyes, and was easily washed out when the embroidery was completed.

Twentieth-century equipment

Material. Use only the best quality, fine white cotton lawn. Do not be tempted to use an inferior quality, as it will only give poor results. Material containing man-made fibres does not respond properly to piercing with the stiletto. The threads of synthetic materials do not part, but instead break, leaving a hole which is difficult to overcast.

Thread. White sewing cotton No. 40. *Not mercerised*. The soft cotton thread used by the 'Flowerers' is no longer available, so a substitute has to be used.

When I began to experiment with threads in the late 1950s, I was still able to obtain white sewing cotton No. 50 and No. 60, but now I understand that only a standard No. 40 is produced. As this is a round thread, I split it lengthwise, as you would with a stranded embroidery cotton, not taking the strands completely apart but just enough to remove the twist. After this treatment, the thread becomes flatter and softer, the stitches blend into each other and the embroidery has a more authentic appearance. This is quite a tedious task to begin with, but, after a little practice, you will become quite adept at it, and when you see the results you will agree it is well worth while. For the needlepoint, drawn fabric and drawn thread work use threads No. 100 and No. 120.

Needles. Crewel size 10. It is advisable to buy a packet of this size as, being so fine, they soon bend or break in use (Fig 53).

Stiletto. Be careful not to buy one with a very sharp point, as this cuts the material and weakens it. The stiletto must only push the threads of the material apart, not break them. If a hole is accidentally made in the wrong place, it should be possible to pull the threads of the material back in to place so that the hole disappears.

Scissors. I like to keep two pairs in use. One pair has very slim blades and sharp points (Fig 53); the other has a protuberance on the point of one blade (Fig 53), and is specially made for cutting the embroidery away from the foundation material. The protuberance prevents accidental snipping of the embroidery.

A sewing ring, not more than 10 cm (4 ins), with the inner ring bound as shown in Fig 53, will be required to work the needlepoint, drawn thread and drawn fabric fillings. Binding the inner ring with a strip of material keeps the lawn taut and prevents it from slipping.

A small magnifying glass (Fig 53) is a very useful piece of equipment when researching and studying pieces of old Ayrshire needlework.

Tracing paper. It is advisable to buy this in a roll rather than in sheets, as you will need to join pieces of the tracing paper with masking

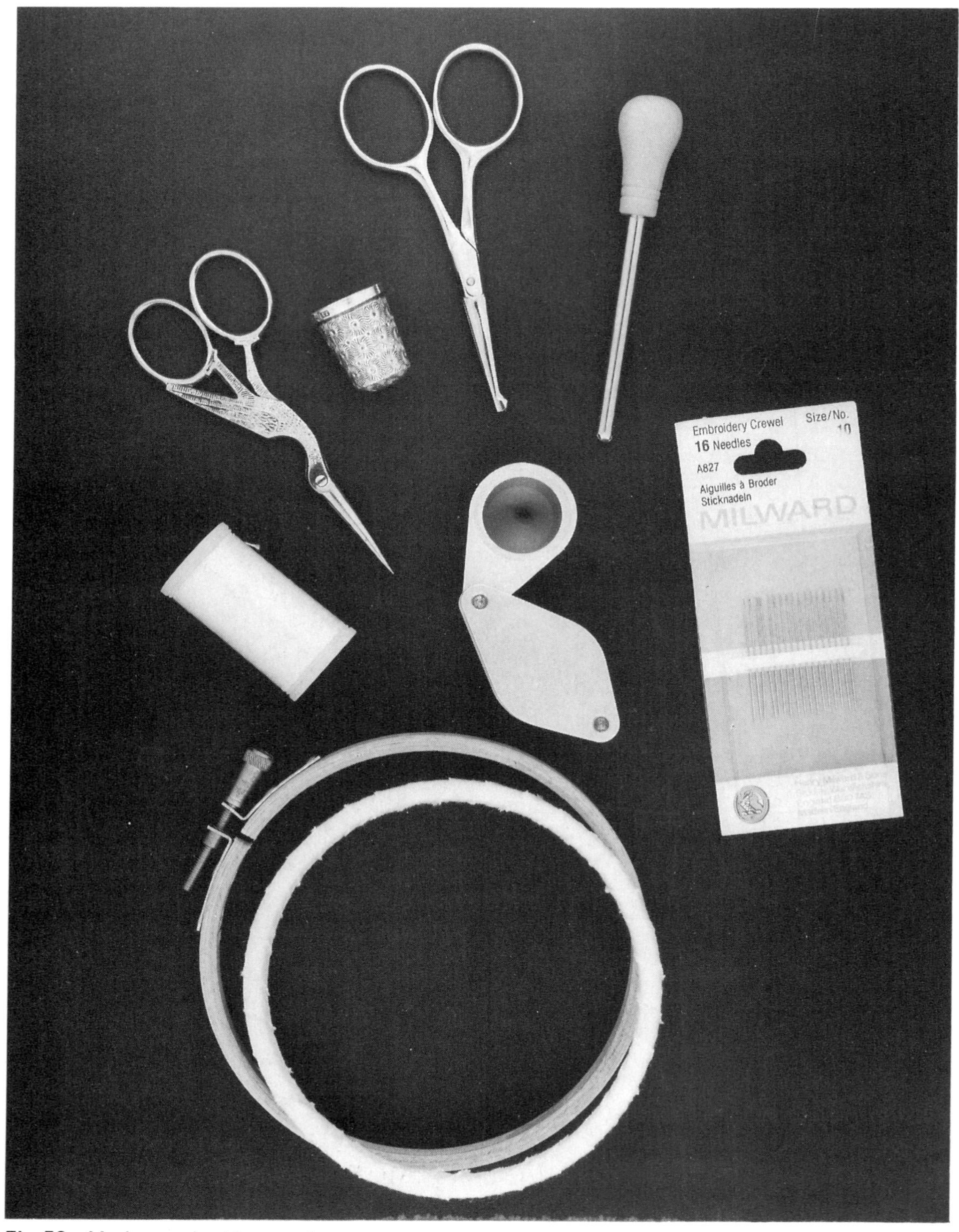

Fig 53 Modern embroidery equipment

tape to make a piece large enough to trace off the pattern for the robe skirt.

Carbon paper. Use a dressmaker's carbon paper, which washes out. It is most important to ensure that this can be done; I always do a test wash. From experience I know how heartbreaking it is to spend many hours on a piece of embroidery and then discover the tracing cannot be removed.

Thimble. I always wear one: 'Flowering' apprentices were not allowed to work a stitch without using one.

Stitches

The names I use for the stitches are the ones passed on to me as having been used by the 'Flowerers', and may differ from those given to similar stitches in other embroidery books.

It is most important that all stitches are kept very small. You might find this difficult when you first begin to work the technique, but no stitch should measure more than 4 mm in length. I strongly recommend that any stitches you intend to use are perfected on a working sampler (Fig 54) before you attempt to incorporate them into your embroidery. If you arrange the embroidery on your working sampler in an organised manner, you will have a second piece of embroidery at no extra cost. One of my students did this, had it framed, and is very proud of her little sampler.

Fig 54 Working samplers

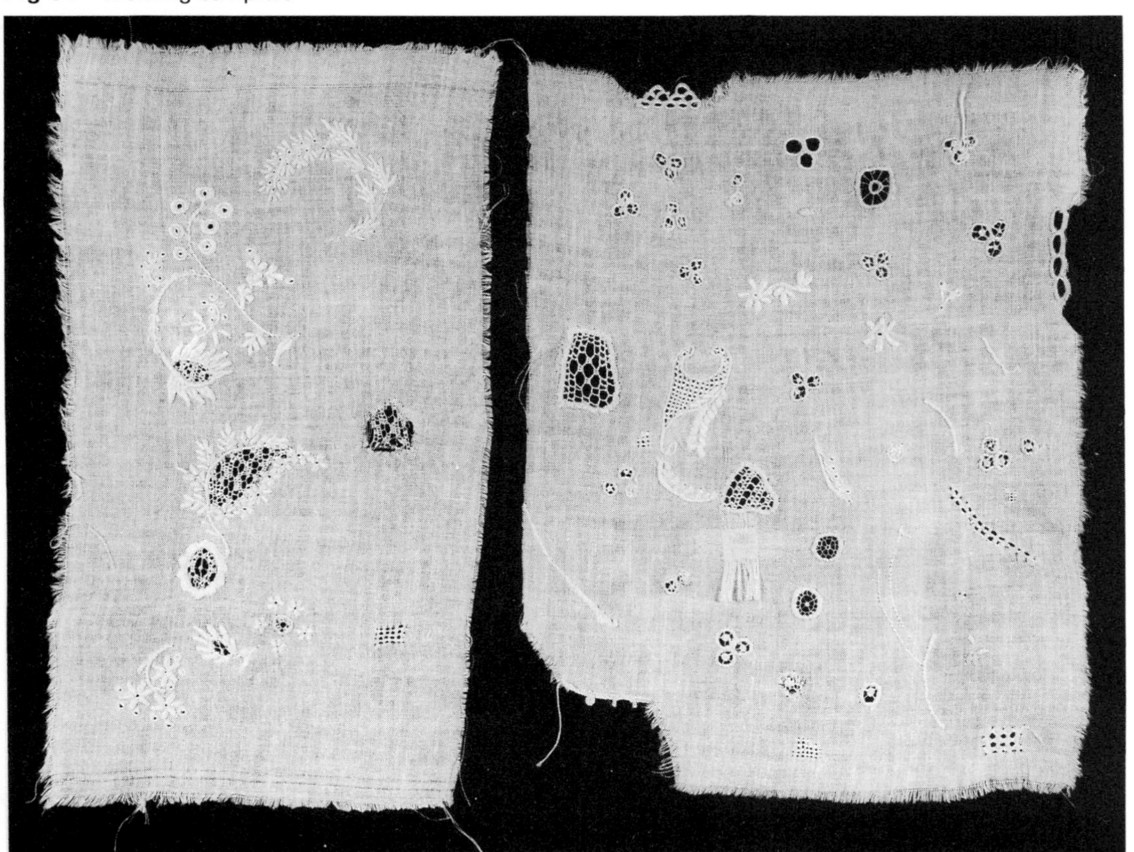

Beading or back stitch

This was used on robes to decorate the casing for the neck and waistline drawstring. Using a double thread in the needle, bring it up from the back about 3 mm from the beginning of the line to be worked, returning it 2 mm along as in Fig 55a. Continue in this manner, bringing the needle up 3 mm ahead of the previous stitch. Keep the stitches even and raised. Do not pull too tightly on the thread.

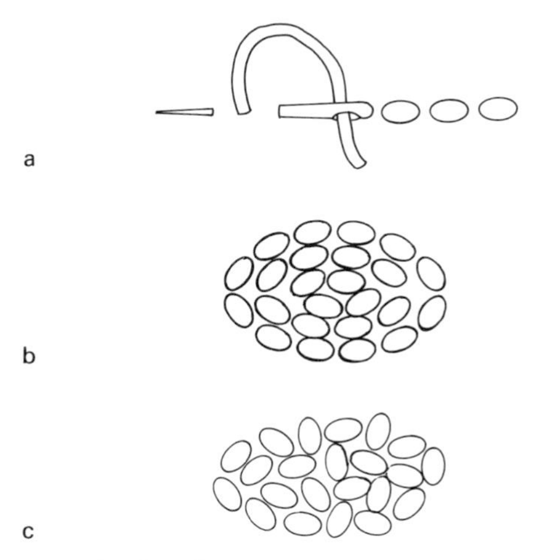

Fig 55 Beading

Back stitch is also used as a filling within an outline or satin stitch, either organised (Fig 55b) or scattered irregularly (Fig 55c). When used in this manner the stitch is called 'Seeding' or 'Powdering'. This stitch was used very cunningly by the 'Flowerers' to speed up their work. Where a row of dots approximately 2 mm in diameter was required, they would work it with 18 to 20 No. 100 threads in the needle. This gives the impression of satin stitch on the surface but is much quicker to work, and it is only when you examine the reverse side that you realise how it was done.

Buttonhole stitch

All the edges in Ayrshire needlework are finished in this stitch, and the surplus material cut away close to the knotted edge of the embroidery.

Work a row of running stitches along the traced line. This strengthens the edge. Working from left to right, bring the needle up on the lower edge of the running stitches and proceed as in Fig 56a, pulling it through over the working thread.

These stitches should not be more than 2 mm in depth and worked as close together as possible, without overlapping, to prevent fraying when the embroidery is cut from the foundation material.

Buttonhole stitch used for scalloping is deeper, up to 4 mm, and requires two rows of running stitches within the traced lines. It is worked as in Fig 56b.

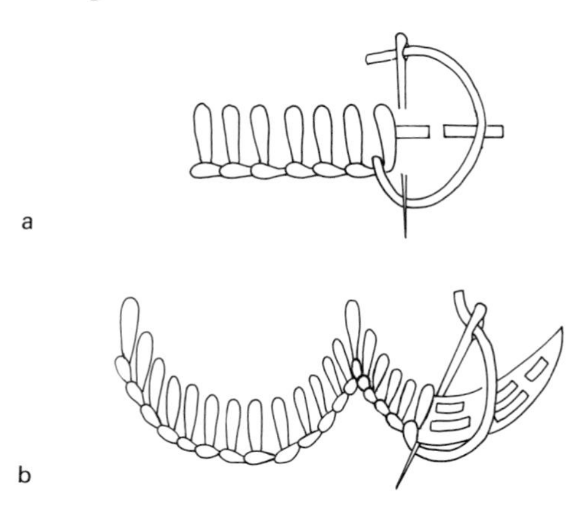

Fig 56 Buttonhole stitch

Cording or outline stitch

An attractive method of working stems and trailing. Also suitable for outlining motifs and working initials.

Work running stitches along the length of the

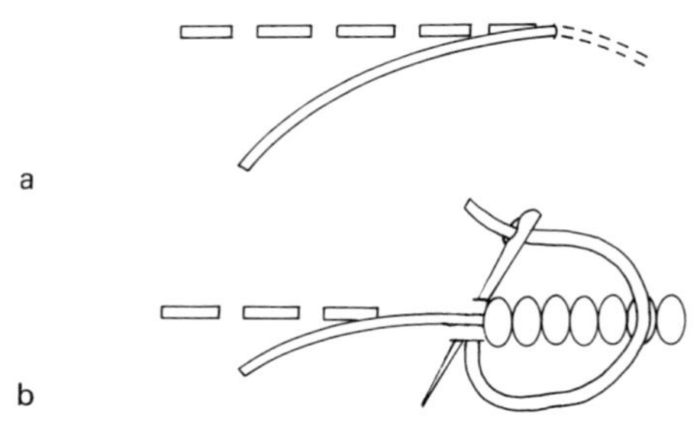

Fig 57 Cording

line to be worked. Bring a second thread up at the beginning of the running stitches, leaving about 1 cm at the back of the work (Fig 57a). Lay this thread on the running stitches and secure by overcasting with very small stitches, taking the needle under the padding thread and running stitches, and picking up only one or two threads of the foundation material (Fig 57b). Finish off by taking the needle back through the last few stitches, on the *surface* of embroidery. Cut off the padding thread close to embroidery and on the reverse side.

Eyelets

Work tiny running stitches close to the traced outline of the eyelet, but taking up only one or two threads of the material, so that as much thread as possible remains on top of the work, forming a padding (Fig 58a). Pierce with the stiletto (Fig 58b). Work around the hole, covering the running stitches with overcasting (Fig 58c). To finish off, pass the needle through a few stitches on *top* of the work (Fig 58d), and cut the thread as close to the embroidery as possible.

For a more delicate eyelet, omit the running stitches. Another variation is to make a small hole with the stiletto and overcast, using a double thread in the needle. This can be seen worked in Fig 49. Always take the needle *down* through the centre of the hole.

To work a continuous line of eyelets, make two journeys in running stitch (Fig 59a) working the full length of the design in a figure of eight pattern, keeping a longer stitch on top of the work and returning to the starting point. Pierce holes with the stiletto.

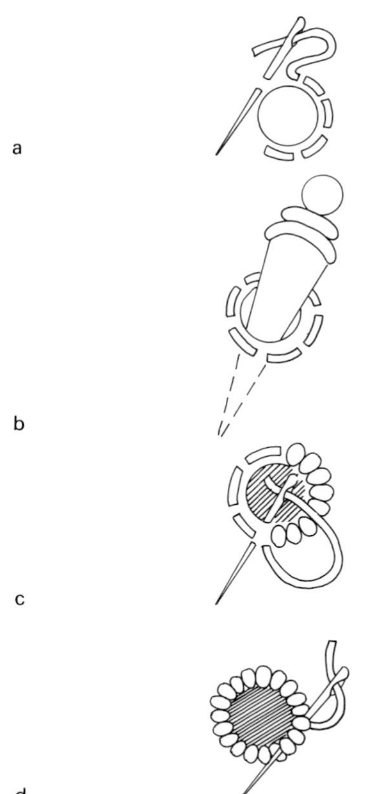

Fig 58 Eyelets

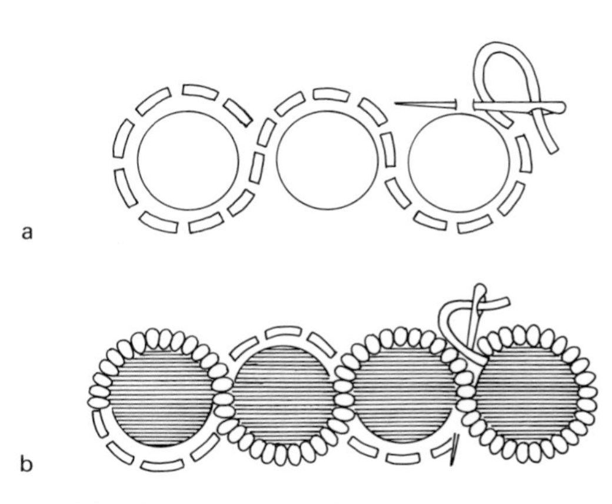

Fig 59 Continuous eyelets

Overcast in a continuous line as in Fig 59b. To improve the shape and appearance of eyelets, bring the tip of the stiletto up through the hole from the back of the completed work.

Oval eyelets

Work running stitches in a figure of eight on a traced line of eyelets (Fig 60a). Cut a slit along the length of the eyelet, being very careful not to cut the thread of the running stitches. Overcast along one side of the eyelets as in Fig 60b. On

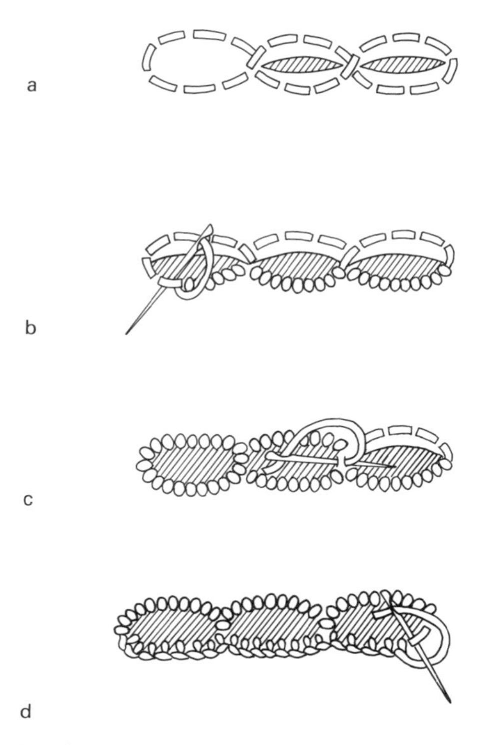

Fig 60 Oval eyelets

Fig 61 Melon seed

the return journey, take the thread around the bar between the eyelets (Fig 60c).

When using eyelets as an edging, work a buttonhole stitch on the return journey (Fig 60d), remembering to take the thread around the bar between the eyelets. Cut the foundation material away along the knotted edge of the buttonhole stitch.

Melon seed

Melon seed is worked by making four running stitch journeys. The first is on the outside of the eyelets; the second is on the inside, as shown in Fig 61a. The third journey completes the outer line, and the fourth the inner line. Working only a few at a time, slit the material along the length of the eyelet, also making a tiny slit mid-way as in Fig 61b. Overcast following the lines of the running stitches, folding the raw edges under with your needle as you proceed (Fig 61b).

Laddering

Laddering, as the name implies, resembles a continuous ladder. In Ayrshire needlework it is not more than 5 mm wide, mostly worked in gently curving lines, as an outline, as veining in leaves and petals, and to lighten more solid fillings, such as satin stitch and seeding.

Work two parallel lines of running stitch, keeping a longer stitch on top, so that the sewing thread forms a padding (Fig 62a). Midway between the lines, make a row of dots 4 mm apart. Commencing at the top of the work, punch holes with a stiletto on the first few dots (Fig 62b). Overcast the edges, starting at the top left-hand corner and working around to the bar between the first two holes (Fig 62c). Now take the thread across to the opposite side and secure (Fig 62d). Work back across, taking the thread around the bridging thread and the material under it (Fig 62e).

To give your work an even and professional finish, *always* take the thread around the bar the same number of times. Continue in this manner until the bottom right-hand corner is reached, then overcast along the bottom and up the other side (Fig 62f). Finish off on *top* of the work by passing the needle through the last few stitches and cutting the thread close to the embroidery.

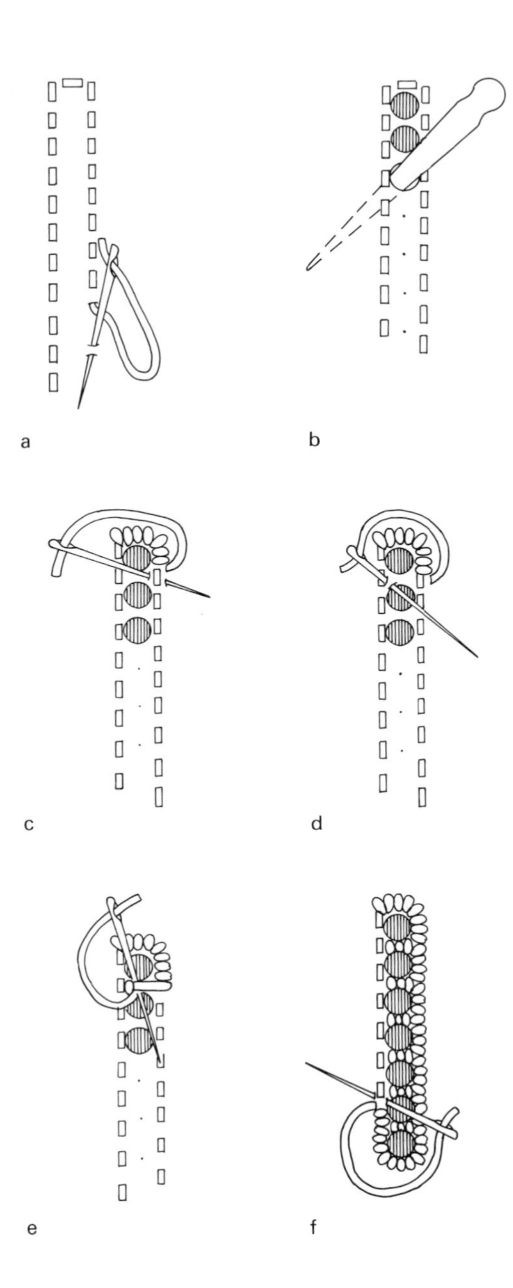

Fig 62 Laddering

Running stitch

Running stitch is worked by bringing the needle and thread up from the back. Carry the thread over 2–3 mm then pick up one or two threads of the material, just enough to secure it. Continue as in Fig 63, keeping as much thread as possible on the surface so that it forms a padding.

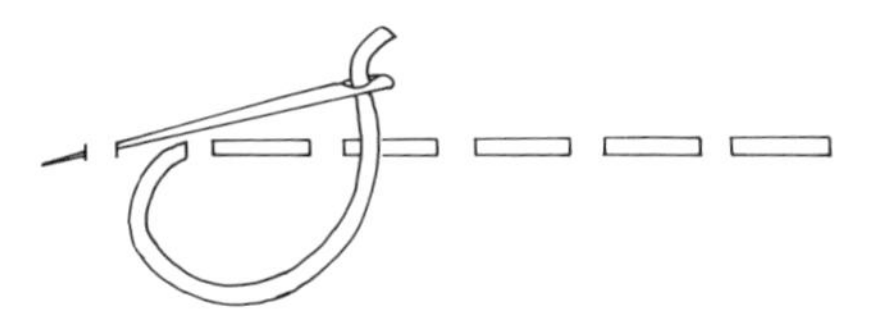

Fig 63 Running stitch

Satin stitch

This is used to work small petals and leaves. Bring the needle and thread through at the bottom of the petal and, taking it to just below the tip, pick up one or two threads of the material (Fig 64a). Return to the bottom and again pick up one or two threads of material (Fig 64b). Repeat, going just beyond the first loop (Fig 64c). Using the same thread and starting from the bottom, work straight stitches horizontally to the tip, taking the needle under the padding and ground material (Fig 64d). Finish off by bringing the needle down between the stitches

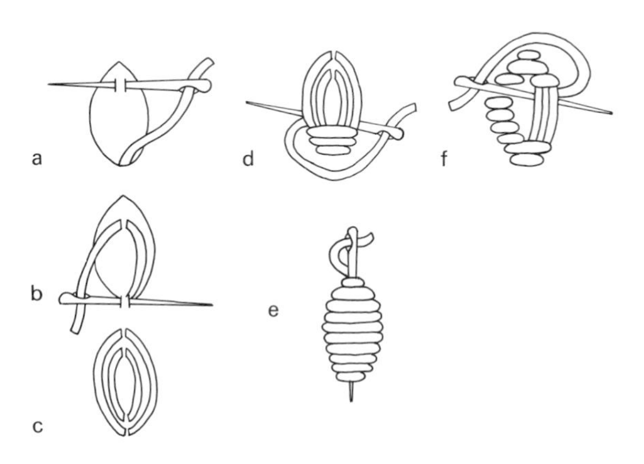

Fig 64 Satin stitch

and material, the length of the petal, on the *surface* (Fig 64e). Cut the thread off close to the embroidery.

An attractive way of working petals is shown in Fig 64f. In Ayrshire needlework the stitches are always worked straight across, never slanted.

Satin stitch dots

These should not measure more than 4 mm in diameter. Because the dots are so small, only three padding stitches are required. Bring the thread up as in Fig 65a. Take it to the opposite side of the circle and pick up a thread of material. Continue as in Fig 65b, keeping all the padding on the surface. Cover padding stitches with straight stitches worked at right angles to them (Fig 65c).

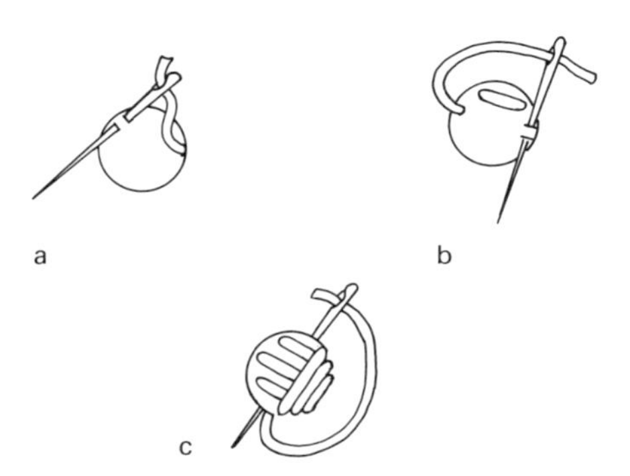

Fig 65 Satin stitch dots

Larger motifs in satin stitch

Pad the area to be worked with running stitches, taking a longer stitch (4–5 mm) on the surface to form a padding. Bring the needle through at the end of the motif on the traced line. Insert it on the opposite side, again on the line; carry it under the motif on the wrong side, and bring it up close to where it first came through. Continue in this manner (Fig 66) until the entire motif has been covered. Finish off on the surface by taking the needle back under the last few stitches.

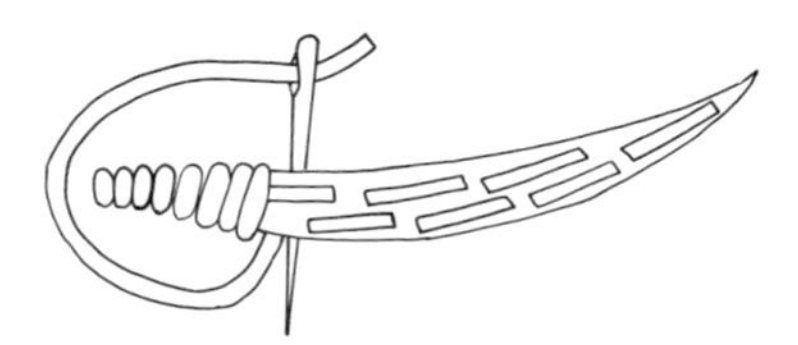

Fig 66 Larger motifs in satin stitch

Stem stitch

In Ayrshire needlework the stitches used in stem stitch must be kept very tiny and regular. Bring the needle up at the beginning of the traced line and, working on the line, make a slanting stitch about 2 mm long (Fig 67).

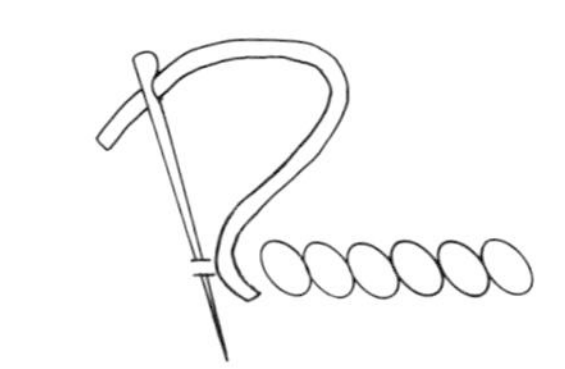

Fig 67 Stem stitch

Four-sided stitch

A counted thread stitch used as a filling in larger spaces. Use a sewing ring or hoop, and No. 120 thread. When working four-sided stitch, I reverse the needle and use it as in Fig 68A. I find the blunt end of a No. 10 crewel needle slips easily between the threads of the material without splitting them. If you use this method you will need to wear a thimble. Note that in Fig 68B the needle is used in the reversed position. Work from right to left.

(1) Count six threads down from the top of the space to be filled, and bring the needle up at **a**. Insert it at **b** six threads above, and bring out

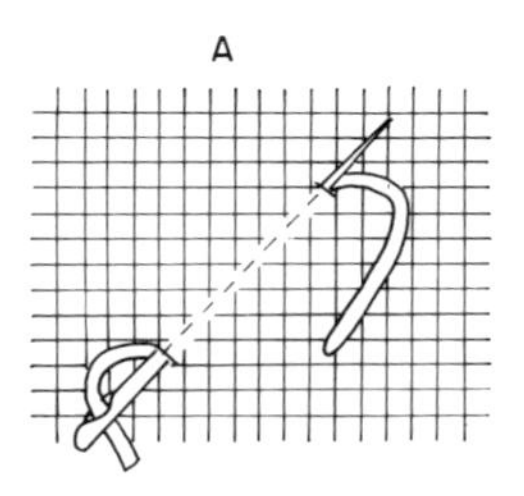

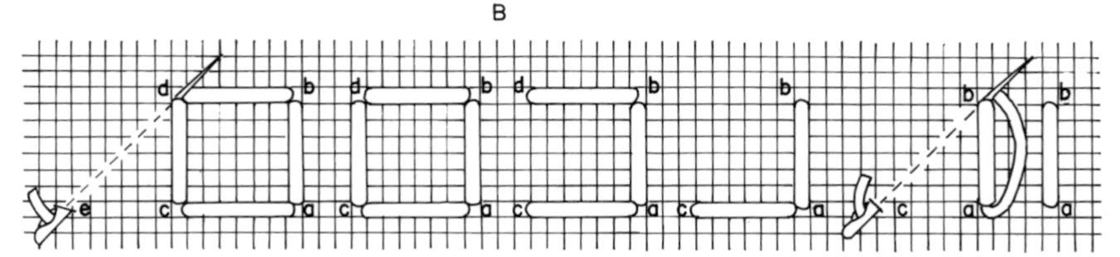

Fig 68 Four-sided stitch

again at **a**. Re-insert at **b** and bring it out six threads to the left and six threads down at **c**.
(2) Insert the needle at **a** and bring it out at **d**, six threads to the left and six threads up.
(3) Insert the needle at **b** and bring it out at **c**. Insert the needle at **d**, and bring it out again at **c**. Re-insert at **d**, and bring it out at **e**, six threads to the left and six threads down.

As you work, pull the thread slightly to open up spaces between the stitches. Following Fig 68B, work to the opposite side of the motif. Turn work around so that the left-hand side of embroidery is now on the right. Bring the needle up six threads below the last hole made on the previous row. Insert the needle into the hole and repeat the first row. Continue in this manner until the space is filled.

Note that you take the thread twice around the vertical threads, and compensate for this on the return journey when you take the thread a second time around the horizontal threads.

When working drawn thread and drawn fabric stitches, I prefer to complete the filling and then work the outline in cording or satin stitch. Working in this order gives a stronger and more clearly defined outline. The 'Flowerers' did the solid embroidery first and then the work was passed to the most experienced embroideresses, who worked the needlelace stitches. This may have been to avoid the delicate fillings being damaged by a less experienced embroideress when working the outline. This filling can be varied by leaving one vertical or one horizontal thread of the material between each little square formed by the four-sided stitch. Another variation is to leave one vertical and one horizontal thread between the squares.

Worked variations of four-sided stitch can be seen on the trunk of the tree and the pomegranates in Fig 44.

Drawn thread network filling

Use No. 120 thread. In the space to be filled, alternately remove three threads and leave three threads, vertically and horizontally. Overcast diagonally on the network of threads produced as shown in Fig 69.

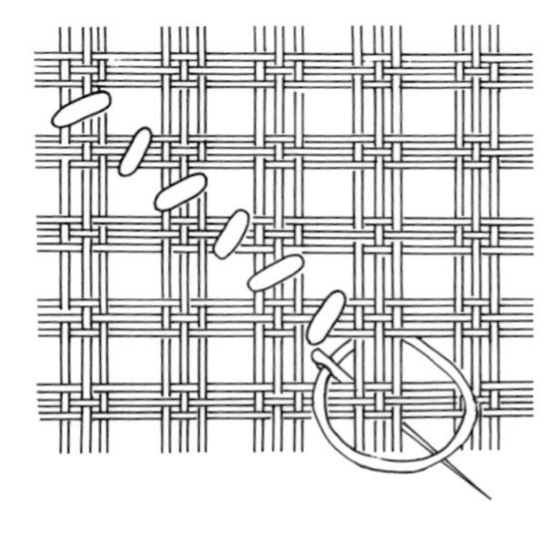

Fig 69 Drawn thread network filling

Eye stitch (worked on a network background)

This stitch gives a very pretty effect when worked on a needlemade net background. Use a single thread of No. 40 or No. 100. No. 100 gives a light, airy effect; No. 40 gives a more solid and prominent result.

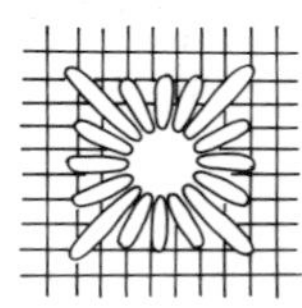

Fig 70 Eye stitch using 16 stitches. Work on a network background

Work sixteen stitches as in Fig 70, working into one central hole but forming a square on the outside edge. Put a slight tension on the stitches to enlarge the hole in the centre. This stitch can be seen worked on a robe in Fig 30. Another version uses 24 stitches arranged as in Fig 71.

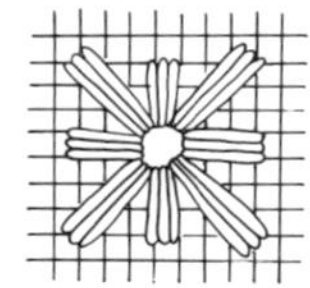

Fig 71 Eye stitch using 24 stitches. Work on a network background

Foundation for needlelace fillings

Use No. 100 thread. This groundwork must be done before the decorative embroidery stitches can be added. Count the threads carefully and adjust at either end so that an even number of vertical bars are obtained. Withdraw vertical threads. Remove five threads and leave two alternately right across the space to be filled. Secure the thread in the traced line above the first two remaining ground threads on left side of work. Bring the needle up two threads down at **a**. Return diagonally across the ground threads and insert at **b**, coming out again four threads down at **c** and inserting it at **d**. Continue in this manner until the opposite traced line is reached. Repeat on each pair of vertical threads. This forms a framework of bars each containing two threads, on which the decorative stitches are worked. In most fillings, only alternate rows of bars are embroidered.

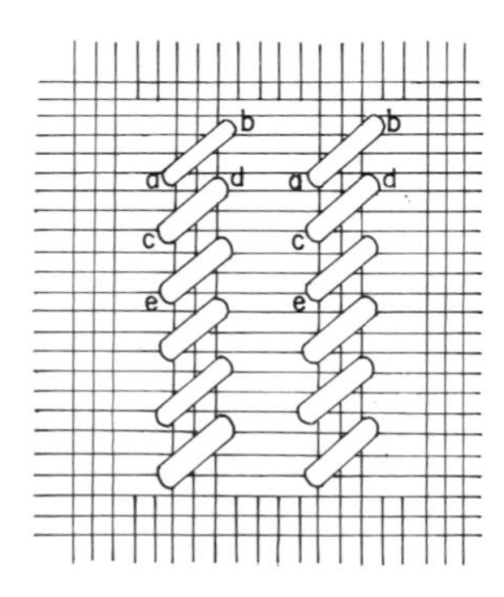

Fig 72 Foundation for needlelace fillings

Feather stitch

Secure the thread on the traced line. Bring the needle up above and just to the left of the centre of the top horizontal bar. Holding the thread down with the left thumb, insert the needle to the right of centre, take it under two bars and pull it up over thread. Turn the thread over and repeat, but inserting the needle to the left of centre. Continue to the bottom of the horizontal bars as in Fig 73. The worked filling can be seen in Fig 77.

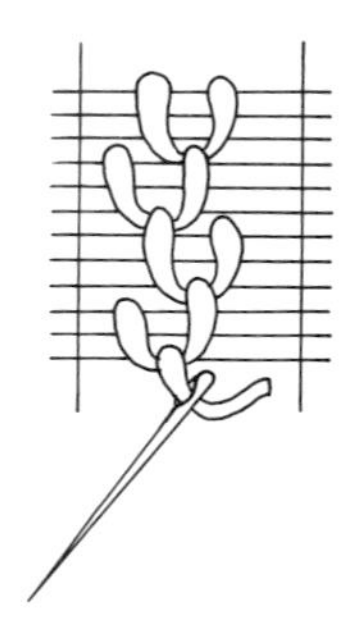

Fig 73 Feather stitch

Overcast bars

Secure the thread on the traced line at the top left-hand side of the group of bars. Take the needle down behind five bars, come up and insert over the first bar. Repeat three more times, working from left to right. Take the needle directly down under ten bars and repeat the first row, but working from right to left. Never take the thread diagonally across the back of the work, as it will show in the finished embroidery. The finished work can be seen in Fig 77.

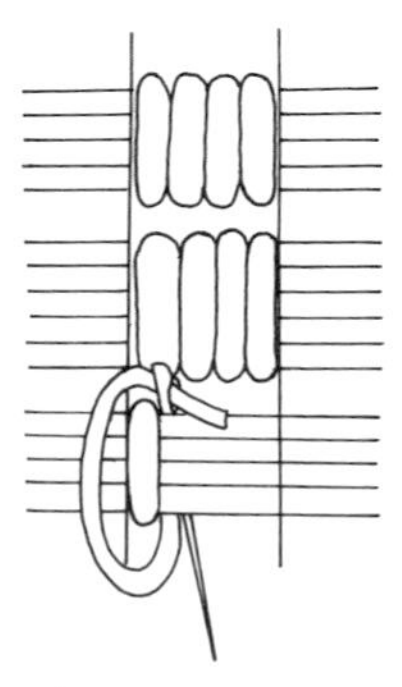

Fig 74 Overcast bars

Variation on overcast bars

This filling is worked diagonally over all the bars. Secure the thread at the top left of the first group of bars. Take the needle down behind four bars, bring it up and insert above first bar. Repeat, but take the thread around five, six, five and four bars. Pass behind the vertical bar to the next row of horizontal bars. Count down eleven bars from the top, bring the needle up under this, and repeat the first group of stitches.

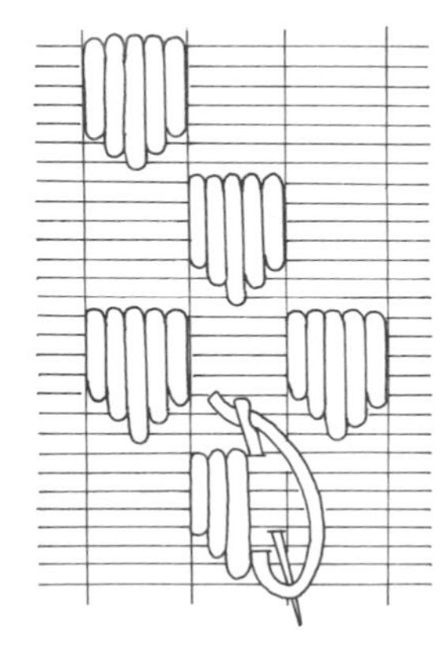

Fig 75 Overcast bars worked diagonally across prepared foundation

Continue in this manner, working diagonally to the bottom right-hand corner (Fig 75). Repeat until the area is completely covered. The worked filling can be seen in Fig 77.

Twisted bars

Secure the thread at centre of a row of horizontal bars. Bring the needle down over the first two bars, return on the left, under the second bar and over the first one. Twisting these two bars

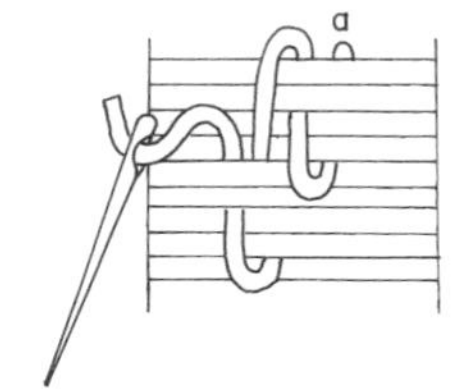

Fig 76 Twisted bars

as you bring the needle up from behind, work above the next bar, and repeat to the bottom of the horizontal bars. This filling can be seen in Fig 77.

Fig 77 Worked fillings

Foundation eyelets for needlepoint fillings

Use cotton sewing thread. The eyelets should be drawn about 1 cm in diameter, but this can be slightly increased or decreased if desired. Work a row of tiny running stitches on the line (Fig 78a,b). Cut away material to 2 mm from running stitches and make small slashes as in Fig 78c. Overcast, overlapping the running stitches with stitches 1 mm to 2 mm in length (Fig 78d), turning the raw edges of the material under with the point of the needle as you work around the hole. Finish off on *top* of the work by taking the needle under the last few stitches. Fig 78e shows the completed eyelet.

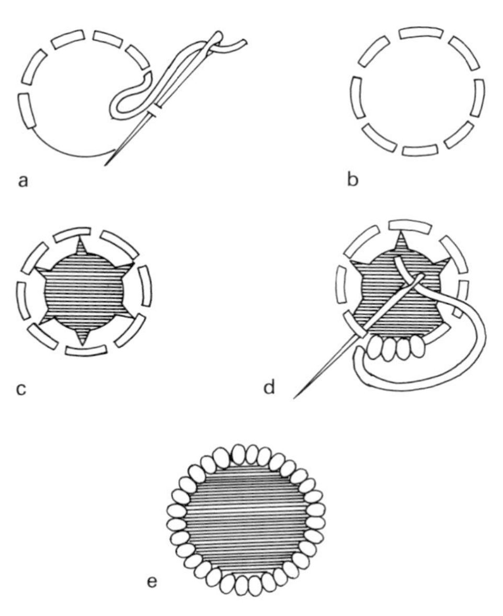

Fig 78 Foundation for round fillings

Eyelet needlepoint filling (1)

Use No. 100 lace thread. To work the twisted buttonhole or lace stitch used for round eyelet fillings follow Fig 79a. Secure the thread in the overcasting, then take the needle under the overcasting, over and under the thread, then pull through till it extends about 2 mm from the overcasting. Work around the circle (Fig 79b) until the space formed by the first buttonhole is reached. Slip the needle through and whip around to the starting point (Fig 79c). Pull up slightly. Continue in this manner (Fig 79d) until the centre is reached, then work to the outside edge by taking the thread around the single thread of the first buttonhole stitch on each round. Finish off in overcasting.

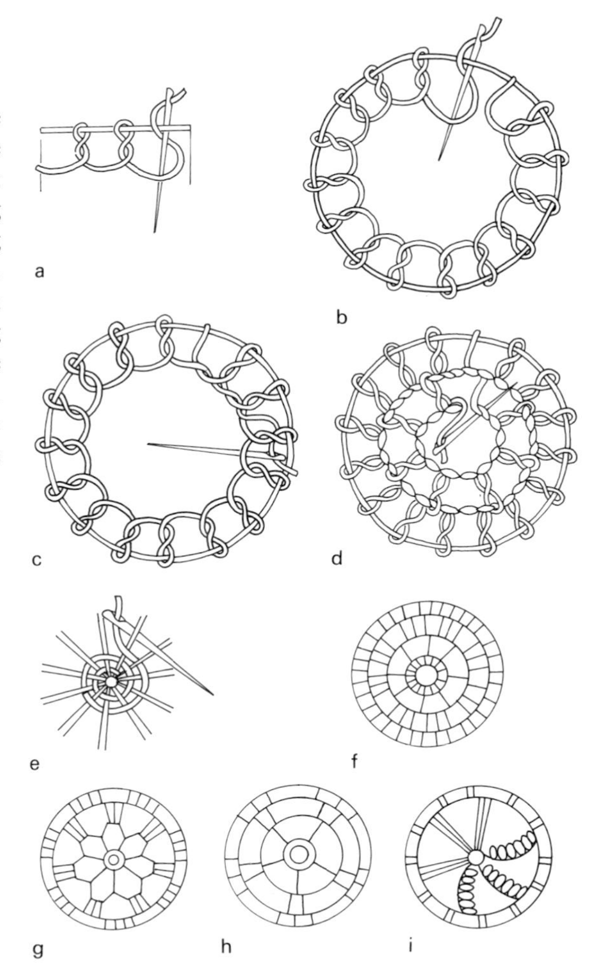

Fig 79 Round needlepoint fillings

For a spider's web (Fig 79e), an odd number of stitches is required so that the thread goes over and under the stitches alternately.

When working needlepoint fillings, the stitches need to be counted as the number of stitches to be worked depends on the filling.

a) (Fig 79f) Work 32 twisted buttonhole stitches; whip around, pulling up slightly. For the second round work a twisted buttonhole stitch into each of the first three spaces, then miss one space. Continue in this manner until the starting point is reached. For the third round, bring the needle up in the first space, miss three stitches and work a twisted buttonhole stitch into the next space. Repeat until the round is completed. Whip, and work a round of tiny buttonhole stitches over the whipping. Whip around by going into the top of each buttonhole stitch and pull up to form a neat circle. Work to the outside edge by taking the thread around the single thread of the first buttonhole stitch of each round. Finish off in overcasting.

b) (Fig 79g) Work 4 twisted buttonhole stitches, then leave a space equal to 4 stitches. Repeat until 7 groups of stitches and 7 spaces have been worked evenly around the eyelet. Whip, going into the top of each buttonhole stitch and twice around the thread over the spaces. For the second round, work three twisted buttonhole stitches into each space, leaving the thread between each group of stitches quite slack. Do not whip on this round. Third round: work one twisted buttonhole stitch into each space, whip and pull up tight. Work a spider's web on the seven stitches, then carry the thread to the outside edge as described for Fig 79f and finish off.

c) (Fig 79h) Work 5 groups of 3 stitches and one space evenly around the eyelet. Whip round, going into the top of each twisted buttonhole stitch and three times around the thread above the spaces. For the second round, make a twisted buttonhole stitch between the first and second and second and third stitches on the first round. Repeat four times and complete the round by taking the needle down through the loop formed by the first buttonhole stitch. Whip, going into the top of each twisted buttonhole stitch and three times around the thread over the spaces. In the third round, work a twisted buttonhole stitch between each group of two twisted buttonhole stitches on the previous round. Whip around twice, and over the whipping work a round of tiny buttonhole stitches. Finish off as described for previous eyelet fillings.

d) (Fig 79i) Work 12 pairs of twisted buttonhole stitches evenly around the prepared eyelet. Into every alternate space work 3 twisted buttonhole stitches, but only pull them up to about 3 mm or 4 mm. Whip round and pull up to a tiny circle. Take the thread out to a space on the first round and work buttonhole stitches back to the centre, grading them so that they are broader in the middle and narrower at each end. Repeat on the other five groups of 3 twisted buttonhole stitches. Take the thread to the outside edge and finish off in the overcasting.

These are only a few suggestions for working needlepoint fillings: there are innumerable permutations in which the twisted buttonhole stitches can be used to fill the eyelets and it is for the embroideress to work out her own permutations, as it was done by the Flowerers.

Eyelet needlepoint filling (2)

Use No. 100 lace thread. Working from the outside of the overcasting (Fig 80a) work 40 buttonhole stitches (note, *not* twisted buttonhole stitch) evenly around the circle and join into the loop formed by the first and second buttonhole stitches with a knot as shown for the whipping in Fig 80b. For this filling the number of buttonhole stitches should be divisible by five.

Work loose buttonhole stitches into every fifth loop (Fig 80a) and join into the first loop with a securing knot (Fig 80b). Whip round, going into each loop, pull up slightly and finish with a knot (Fig 80b). Take the needle back to where the first loop of the second round came up. Start weaving over and under the threads of the second round of buttonhole stitches, getting broader on the inside edge to form peaks, as shown in Fig 80c. Work a round of twisted buttonhole stitches, working into the spaces between each peak and whip round. Pull up, knot and weave the thread to the outside edge and finish off in the overcasting by taking the needle under a few stitches on top of the embroidery.

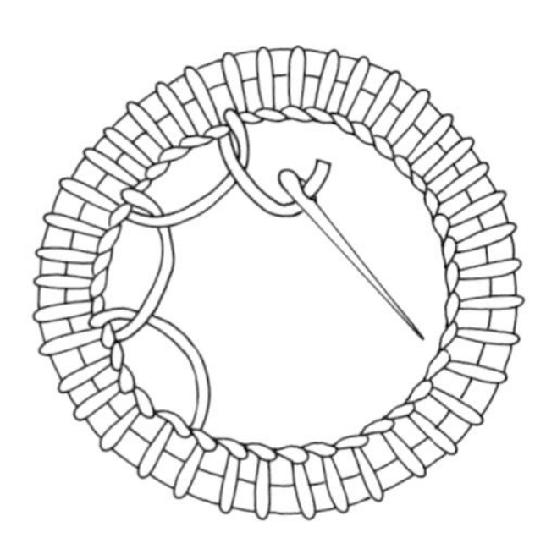

a

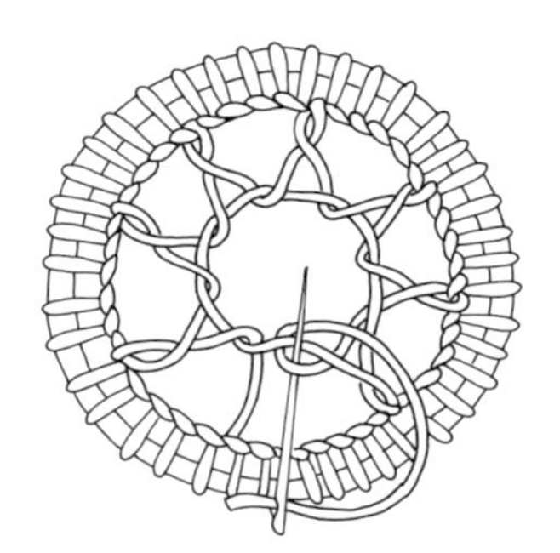

b

c

Fig 80 Needlepoint fillings

12 Traditional Ayrshire needlework christening robe

The pattern included in the book is intended to be used as a guide to the style of the traditional Ayrshire needlework christening robe. It is for the embroideress to work out her own design to give her robe individuality.

The design on the pattern is intended to make it easy for the embroideress with little or no experience of designing to trace off and embroider. Some blank spaces have been incorporated in the design, so that the initials and the date of either birth or baptism of each child baptised in it can be added (Fig 82).

All the bodice pieces are exactly as on a traditional robe, but I have cheated a little on the skirt. Because of the many hours I have spent pressing old robes with voluminous tubular skirts, I designed this one to open right down the back, so that it can be laid out flat for ironing. This reduces considerably the time and patience needed to launder it. A long underskirt should be worn under this garment to prevent small legs from popping out between the buttons.

Materials

2 m fine cotton lawn
300 m Coats cotton sewing thread (*not* mercerised)
No. 100 lace thread
Crewel needles, size 10
Stiletto
A small sewing ring (10 cm)
Tracing paper (greaseproof paper may be used)
Dressmaker's tracing paper
Masking tape
5 small buttons
2 m x 6 mm cotton tape

Method

Trace off all the pieces on the pattern. Turn the right side of the skirt **2R** over and retrace for **2L**. Check that you have *right* and *left* sections of the skirt before starting to transfer the design on to the material. Join the stitching lines (- - - -) along the top of the skirt sections **2R** and **2L**. Lay out all the pieces as in Fig 83 or according to the dimensions of your material, keeping to the grain of the fabric.

To transfer the tracing to the material, the dressmaker's tracing (carbon) paper should be placed with the 'carbon' side next to the material and between the tracing and the material. Pin the tracing securely to the material. Care should be taken that the pins which hold the design in position do not go through the dressmaker's tracing paper, as they will leave marks. For the outline of the skirt, the dressmaker's tracing paper will need to be cut up into long strips and joined together with masking tape to make a piece large enough to fit under the design on the front panel.

The lines of the design should then be firmly drawn over with a pencil or a fine line pen. If using a pencil, keep the point very sharp. I like to use a pencil to trace off the design, and then a coloured pen for transferring it to the material, so that I can see exactly which pieces of the design have been traced. The impression on the material should have very fine lines, not heavy and thick ones. After tracing off all the pieces, remove the tracing and the carbon paper.

Work running stitches along all the broken lines (- - - -). It is most important to follow these lines exactly, as they become the guidelines for assembling the robe and will also allow you to

Fig 81 Traditional Ayrshire needlework christening robe (worked by the author)

Fig 82 Embroidered initials (worked by the author)

launder your embroidery before you start to assemble it. The pieces are much easier to fit together if they have been washed and ironed. Soiled work should not be pressed, as the hot iron may 'set' stains and make them impossible to remove. I recommend that you wash all the pieces at once, in the same solution, no matter how tempted you are to see each piece laundered as you finish embroidering it. It is amazing how many different shades of white can be produced when using modern biological washing products.

At this stage I cut the material into workable pieces, leaving a good margin around all the designs.

Embroider all the pieces, using the stitches described in Chapter 11. All the embroidered edges must be worked with tiny buttonhole stitches laid close together to prevent fraying when cutting the embroidery from the foundation material. Make the buttonholes where indicated on the pattern (**x**). The buttonholes must be made in proportion to the size of the

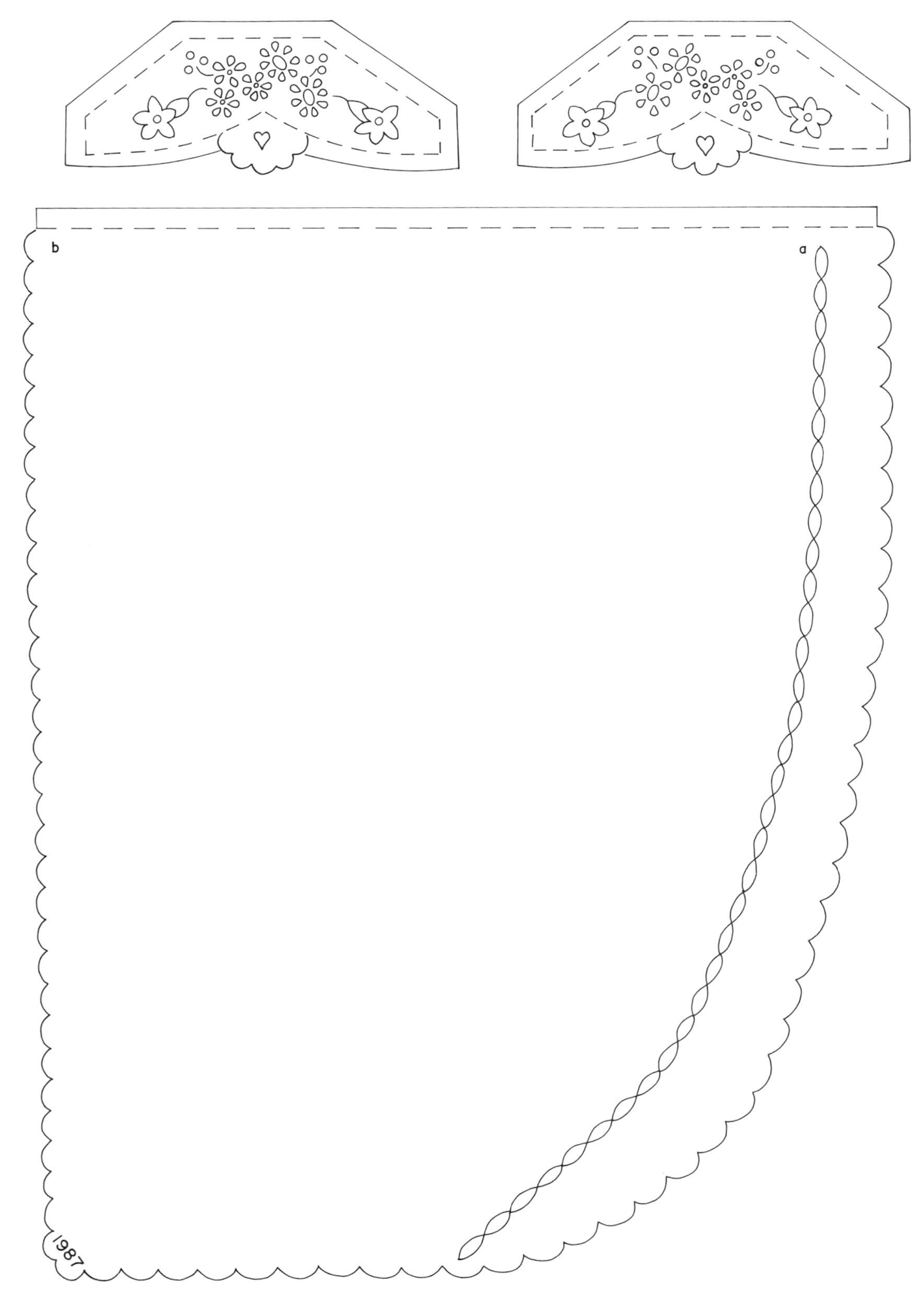

Fig 83 Layout of traced designs on the material

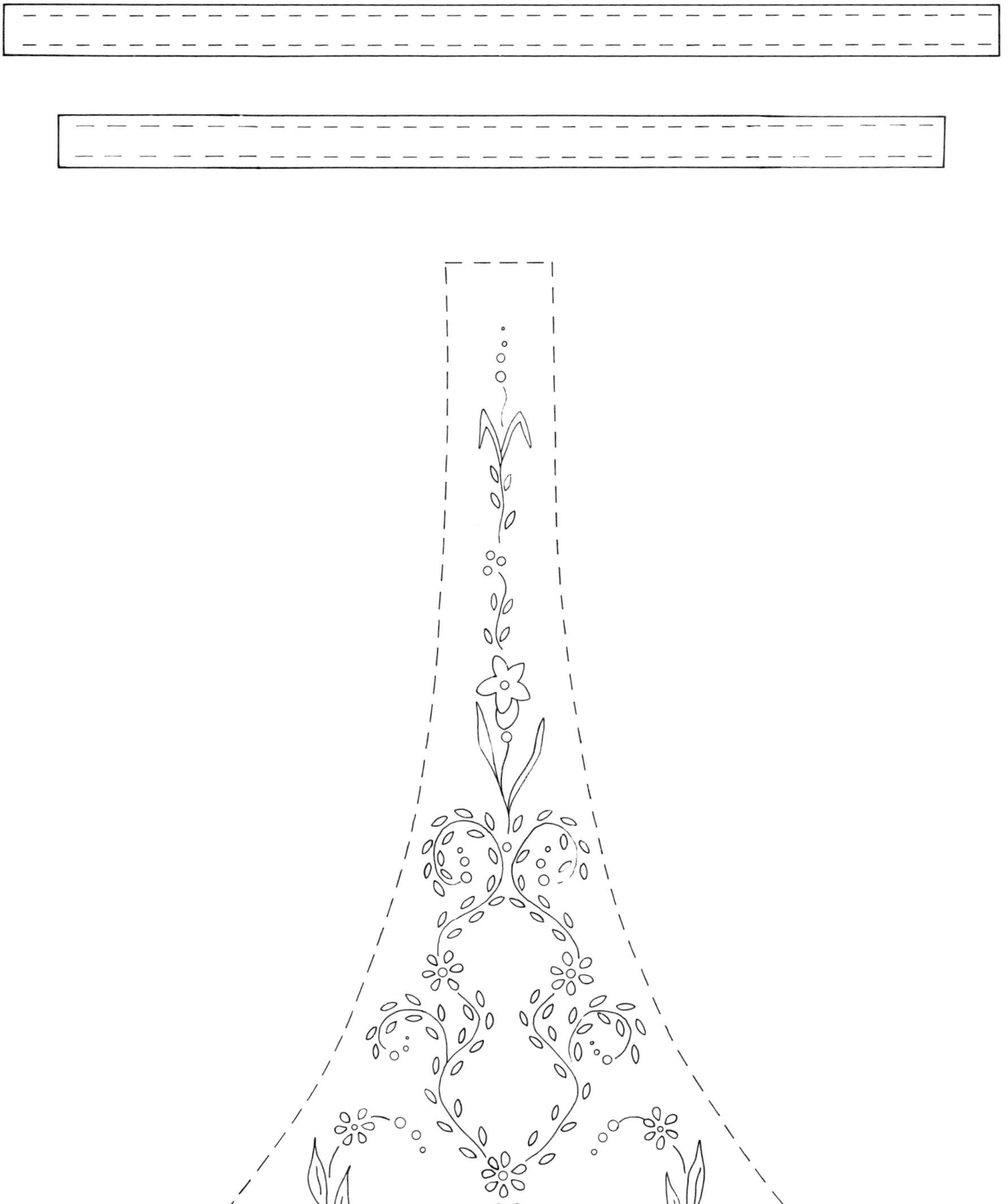

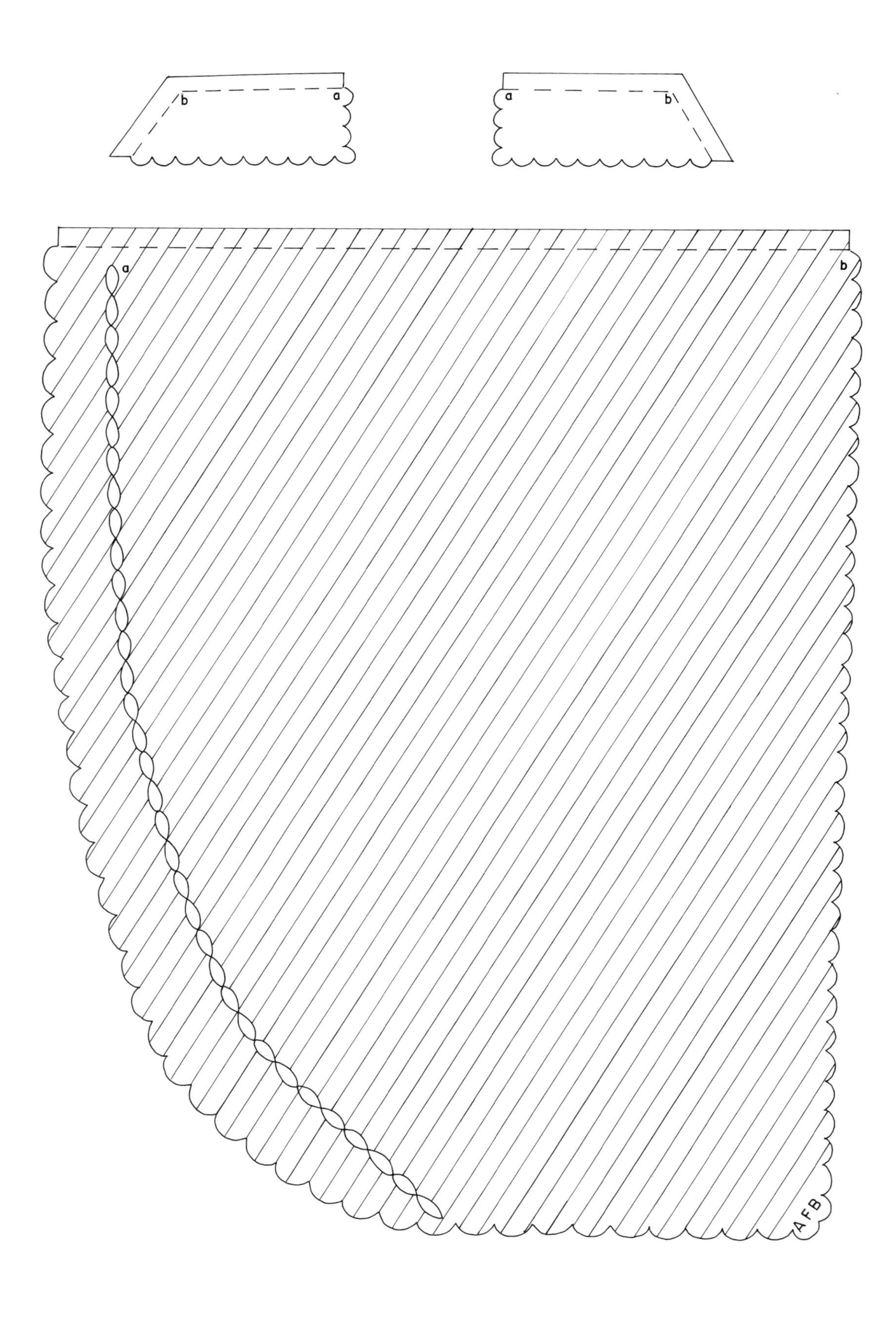

b
a
a
b
a
b
AFB

a
b
a
a
b
b
a
b
b
b
a
a

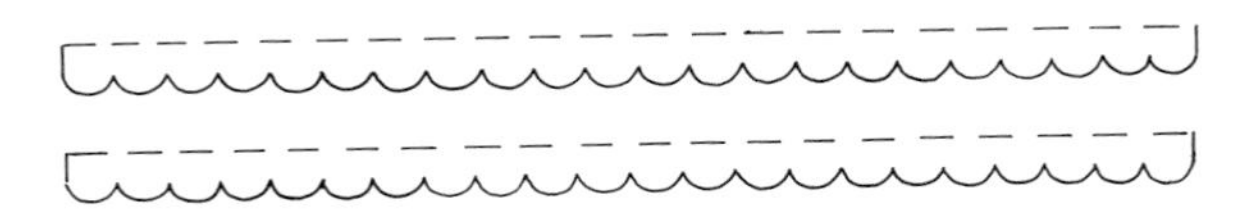

buttons to be used. Measure the length of slit which will be required to accommodate the button and mark on material.

Buttonhole

Work running stitches around the mark as shown in Fig 84a. Carefully cut a slit along the length of the mark. Work along the top edge (Fig 84b) using buttonhole stitch. When the end of the slit is reached, work two long stitches as shown in Fig 84c. Turn the work around and repeat along the bottom edge. The finished buttonhole is shown in Fig 84d.

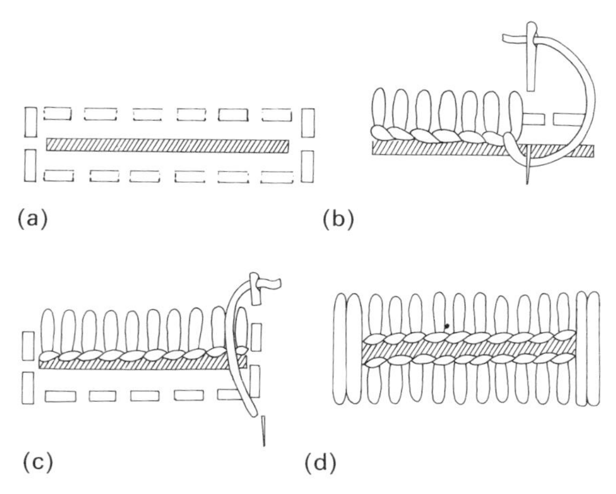

Fig 84 Buttonhole

After embroidering the scalloped edge of the skirt panels **2L** and **2R**, cut them away from the foundation material, leaving a 1 cm margin along the top edge above the stitched line. Cut the foundation material away from the scalloping on the bottom edge of the panel **1**.

Lay skirt pieces **2L** and **2R** on panel **1** matching the tips of the scallops on the skirt to the stitched lines on the panel. Pin in place and secure by tacking along the line of the eyelets. Starting from the bottom edge, work running stitches in a figure of eight along the full length of the eyelets, returning to the starting point and working through both layers of the material. Remove the tacking stitches. Work the oval eyelets as in Fig 60. (I would recommend that you perfect working the oval eyelets on your sampler, using two thicknesses of material, before you apply them to your embroidery.) Very carefully, cut away the surplus material from the reverse of the panel.

Assembling the robe

Wash all pieces. Iron on the wrong side and cut away any surplus material from the embroidered edges of the bodice, including the wings, peak and the scalloped embroidery on the sleeves. Leaving an 8 mm to 1 cm margin on all stitched lines (- - - -), cut the pieces from the foundation material (Figure 86).

On the bodice front (**3**) place the 'wing', flat frill, **6L** as shown in Fig 87, with the sewing lines and right sides together. Work a line of tiny running stitches from **a** to **b**, through both layers of the material, to secure the 'wing'. Cut away surplus material to 3 mm from running stitches.

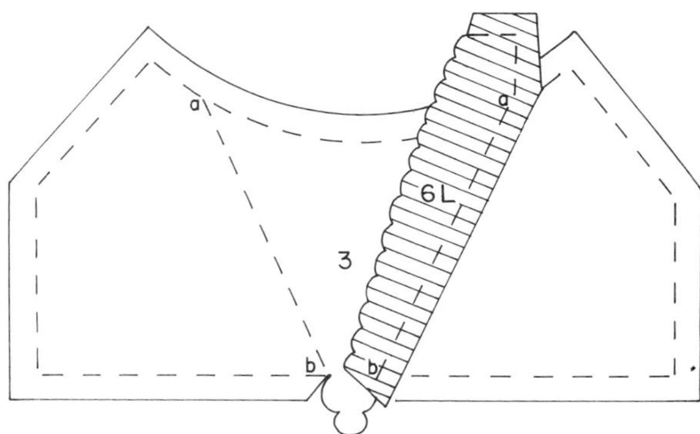

Fig 87 Attaching 'wing' to bodice

Fold **6L** back over running stitches and tack in position on the stitched line at the top of the raglan edge and on the neckline. Join **6R** to bodice **3** in the same manner. Bring the peak out on top of the 'wings'.

To gather the back wing **7L**, secure the thread by taking three back stitches on top of each other at the scalloped edge, 2 mm above the

Fig 85 Embroidered front panel

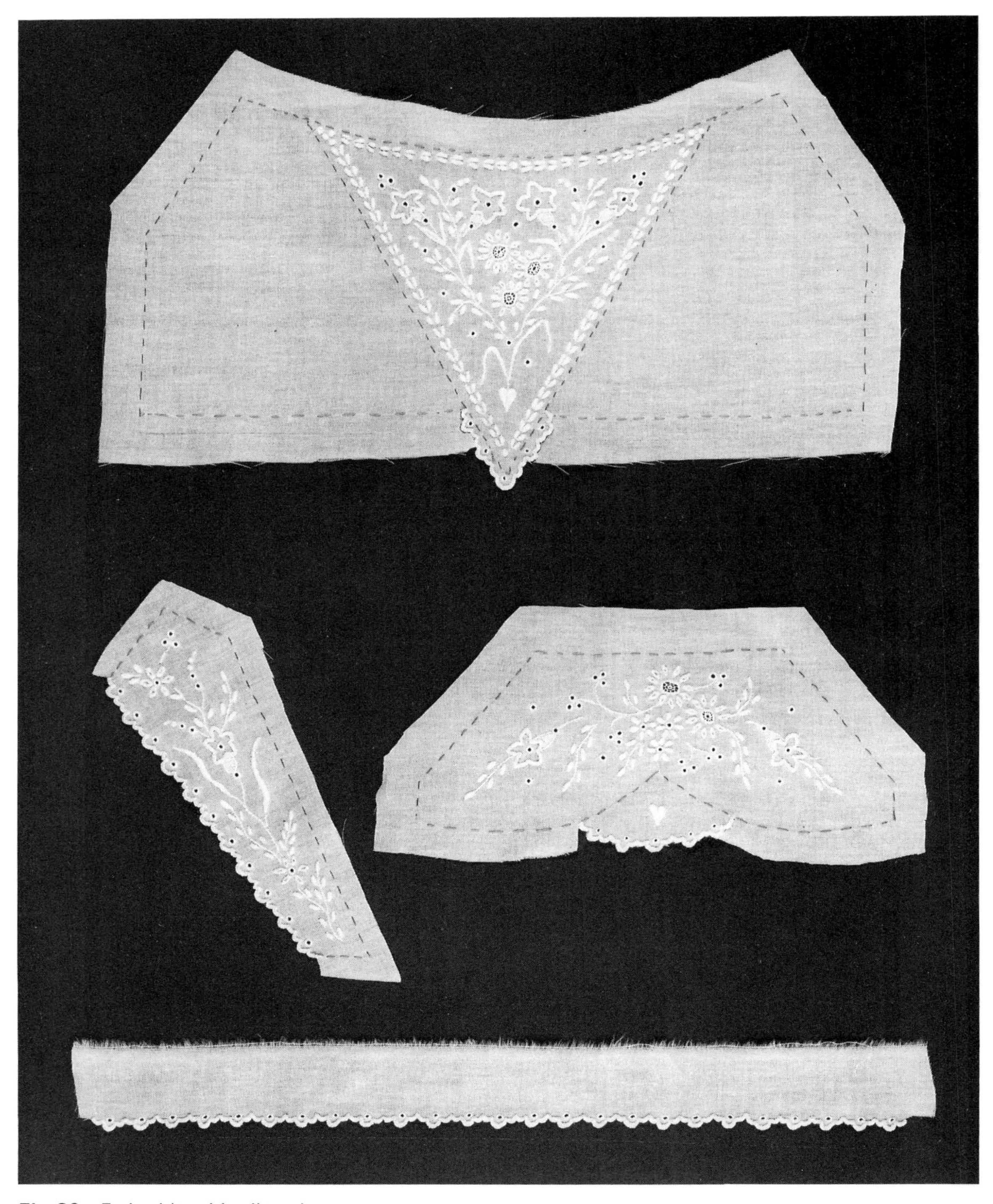

Fig 86 Embroidered bodice pieces

Fig 88 Reverse of robe showing placement of back 'wings'

Fig 89 Diagram showing the layout of the bodice sections

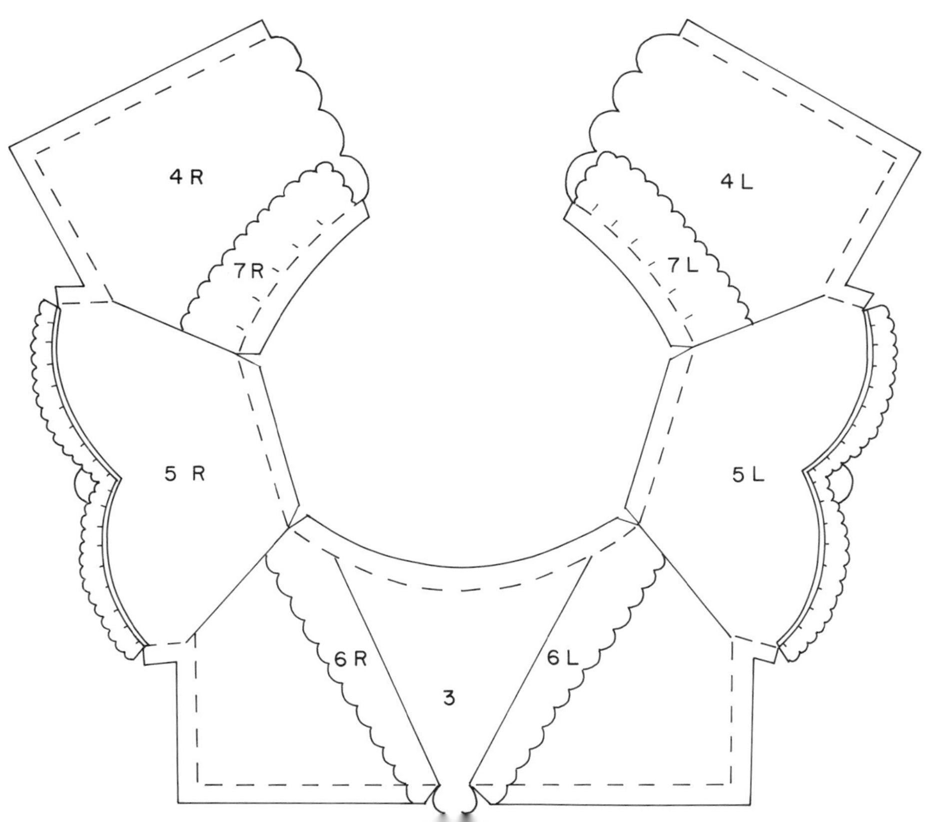

stitched line. Keeping 2 mm above the stitched line, work a row of running stitches from **a** to **b** **7L**. Draw running stitches up evenly to fit from **a** to **b** on **4L**. Fasten the thread off securely. Place **7L** on **4L**, matching **a** to **a** and **b** to **b**. Tack in place on the stitched line, along the neckline and down the raglan edge of the bodice for the depth of the wing. Attach **7R** to **4R** in the same manner.

Attach frill to sleeve. Work gathering stitches on the stitched line on one of the scalloped edgings (**8**). Find the middle of edging and pin in place on the centre point of the stitched line on the sleeve **5R**, where the curved lines meet. Draw up gathering stitches to fit the curved lines and fasten the thread off. Tack in position, fitting the stitched line on the frill over the curved stitched lines on the sleeve. Secure by working two rows of tiny back stitches laid close together on the stitched line. Cut away surplus material on the frill, close to the stitching. Cover the back stitches and raw edge with buttonhole stitches, about 2 mm deep, with the 'knotted' edge of the buttonhole stitches towards the scalloped edge of the frill, going through all the layers of material. Cut away surplus foundation material from under the frill. Attach the frill to **5L** in the same manner.

Join sleeves to bodice pieces as shown in Fig 89, using French seams. French seam: place two appropriate pieces *wrong* sides together and tack along the stitched line. Work a line of tiny running stitches 4 mm from the stitched line on the cut edge side (Fig 90a). Cut away surplus material to 2 mm from the running stitches. Remove the tacking stitches. Turn over to the wrong side, so that the *right* sides of the material are facing. Tack in place and secure with tiny running stitches on the stitched line (Fig 90b).

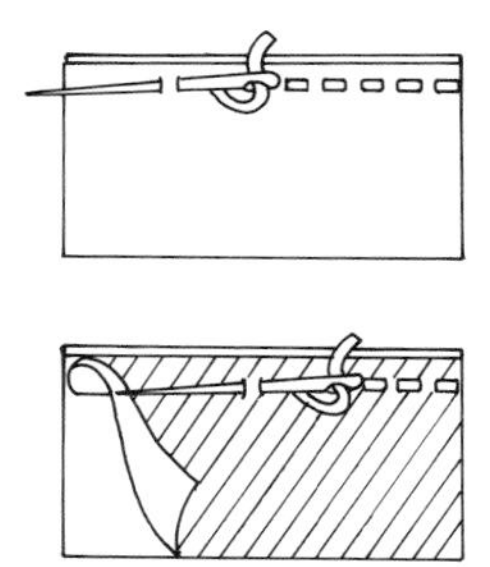

Fig 90 French seams

Now join the sleeve and side seams in the same manner. Do not join the lace edges: they should be left free.

Work gathering stitches on the stitched line of the skirt **2L** from **a** to **b.** *Do not gather over the 'wings' (flat frills).* Draw up to fit the lower edge of the bodice, spreading the gathers evenly. Repeat on **2R**.

Gather the top of the front panel **1** very slightly to fit under the peak and pin in position. Lay the skirt sections on *top* of the bodice, right sides up, with the stitched lines on the bodice and the skirt 8 mm apart. Pin in place and tack. Midway between the stitched lines, join the bodice securely to the skirt with tiny back stitches. Cut away surplus material from the top of the skirt sections, close to the back stitches.

To make the waistband, cut a piece of material on the straight, 52 cm long and 1.6 cm wide. Fold 5 mm under at each end and 3 mm along each side the length of the waistband. Press and tack. Make a 4 mm vertical buttonhole 1 cm from one end and 3 mm from each edge. Match up the buttonhole end of the waistband to the scalloped edge and over the join of back bodice **4R** and skirt **2R**. Keeping the top edge of the waistband on the stitched line of the bodice, tack in place on the waistline.

Work a line of beading stitches between 1 mm and 2 mm from the top edge of the waistband, going through all the layers of material. *Omit the section over the top of the panel.* Repeat the beading between 1 mm and 2 mm from the lower edge, but this time working along the whole length of the waistband. Remove stitched line threads.

For the casing to the waistband cut a piece of material on the straight, 52 cm long and 1.4 cm wide. Fold 5 mm under at both ends and 3 mm along both sides of casing. Press and tack. Slip-stitch to the reverse side of the waistband, taking care that the stitches do not show on the right side. Remove tacking threads.

Work beading stitches under the peak, going through both waistband and casing. Leave the peak detached, so that it can be worn in the

Above **Fig 91** Bodice showing the 'peak' over the waistband to indicate a boy

Fig 92 Bodice with the 'peak' tucked in behind the waistband for a girl

traditional manner – over the waistband for a boy (Fig 91), and tucked in behind it for a girl (Fig 92).

Neckline

On the frill (**9**) work a line of gathering stitches 1 mm from the stitched line on the side away from the scalloped edge. Pull up slightly to fit the neckline of the bodice and fasten off the thread. Lay the frill on *top* of the neck edge of the bodice, right sides up, and the stitched lines 5 mm apart. Tack in position. Secure with back stitches midway between the stitched lines. Trim back surplus material on the frill, close to back stitches.

For the neckband, cut a piece of material on the straight, 60 cm long and 1.4 cm wide. Fold under 5 mm at each end and 3 mm on the long sides. Press and tack. Make a vertical buttonhole, 4 mm long and 2 mm in from each edge, 1 cm from one end of the neckband. Place the buttonhole end of neckband on scalloped edge of **4R** and, keeping the fold of the neckband just above the stitched line on the frill, tack in position. Work a line of beading between 1 mm and 2 mm from the edge along both sides of the neckband, going through all layers of material.

To make the casing for the neckband, cut a piece of material on the straight, 60 cm long and 1.2 cm wide. Fold 5 mm under at both ends and 3 mm on the long sides. Press and tack in position on the reverse side of the neckband. Slip-stitch along both sides, being careful not to take stitches through to the right side of the neckband. Cut two pieces of tape, 80 cm for the neckline and 76 cm for the waistband. Thread the tape through the waist and neck bands, taking the bodkin in at the vertical buttonholes. Hem the tape ends to prevent fraying.

Sew buttons in place to correspond with buttonholes.

13 Handkerchiefs

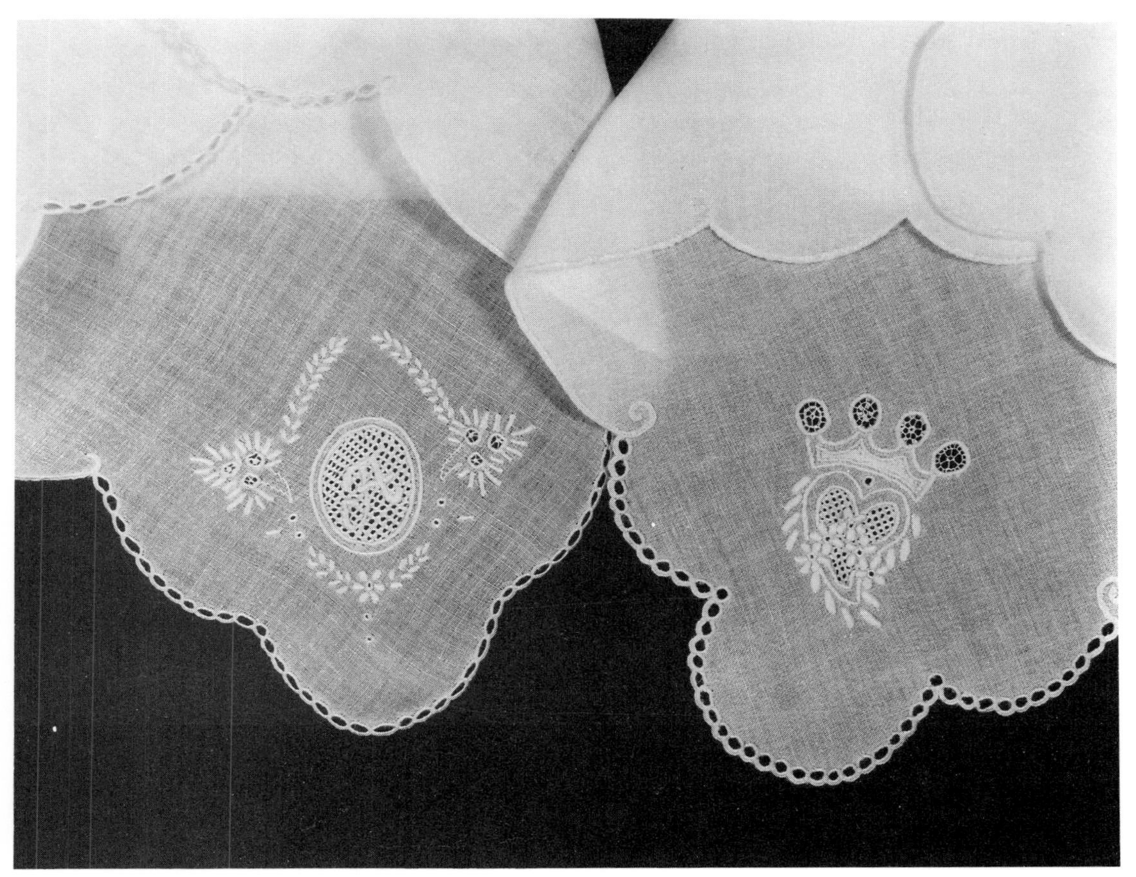

Fig 93 Two handkerchiefs worked from the basic pattern (Fig 94). An initial with a drawn fabric background is worked on the handkerchief on the left. The one on the right shows an adaptation of the Scottish Women's Rural Institutes badge. The needlepoint fillings replace the letters SWRI and the flowers the words 'For Home and Country' (worked by the author with kind permission from the SWRI)

Materials

A piece of fine cotton lawn 30 cm square
Reel of sewing cotton. If needlepoint fillings are to be worked, a small quantity of No. 100 lace thread will also be required
A No. 10 crewel needle
Tracing paper
Dressmaker's tracing paper
Handkerchief pattern (Fig 94)

Fig 94 Basic pattern for a handkerchief

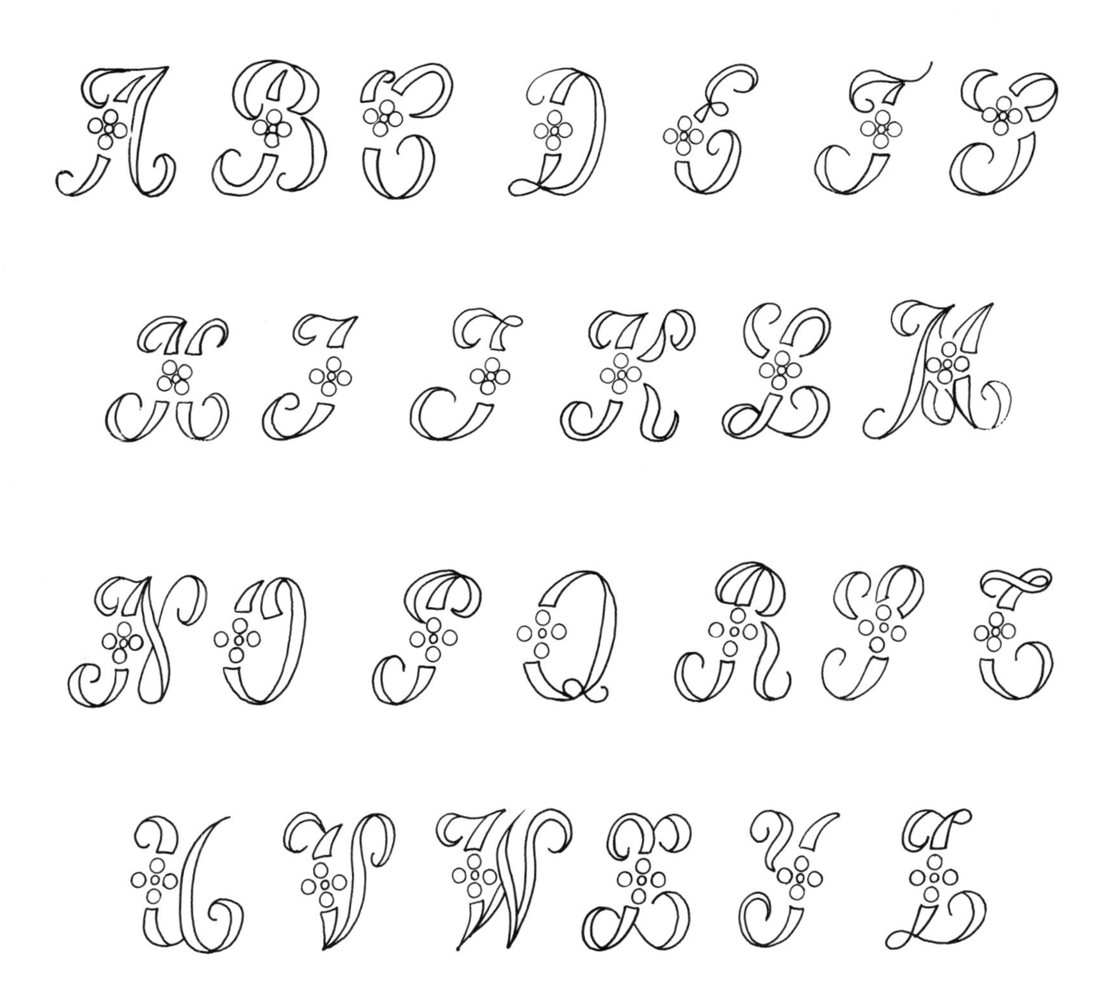

Fig 95 Initials suitable for Ayrshire needlework

Method

To make the handkerchief pattern, trace off the pattern pieces in Fig 94 on separate pieces of tracing paper. Join **A** to **A**, **B** to **B**, **C** to **C** and **D** to **D**, using masking tape. At this stage it is advisable to retrace the joined-up pattern so that a more permanent copy is obtained.

For an initialled handkerchief, trace off the required initial (Fig 95) in the corner with the eyelets. To give an authentic Ayrshire needlework appearance, add a simple design of flowers and leaves. Lay the tracing on the material, checking that it is on the grain of the fabric, and trace off using the method described for the christening robe. Using the sewing cotton, work the initial in well padded satin stitch, keeping all the padding on top of the work. For the scalloped edges, use tiny buttonhole stitches over running stitches (Fig 56a), laid very close together to prevent fraying when the surplus material is cut away. The eyelets are worked as described for oval eyelets (Fig 60d), keeping the knotted edge of the stitch to the outer edge of the design. Wash and press. Cut away from the foundation material.

The second handkerchief (Fig 93) shows how easy it is to work out a design. I simply adapted the Scottish Women's Rural Institute badge to a design suitable for Ayrshire needlework. I replaced the letters SWRI with needlepoint filled eyelets and the words 'For Home and Country' with five small flowers. The stitches used are cording, eyelet, four-sided, satin stitch and seeding. The solid embroidery is worked with cotton sewing thread; the large eyelet fillings and four-sided stitch with No. 100 lace thread. This design is very popular with SWRI members.

14 Pincushions and invitation card

A pincushion makes a lovely gift and, although it may never be used for the purpose for which it was originally intended, it will be even more treasured by the recipient if it has been specially designed and worked by the embroideress.

Square pincushion

Materials

Two pieces of fine cotton lawn 15 cm square
Reel of sewing cotton. If needlelace fillings are to be used, a small quantity of No. 100 lace thread will be required
No. 10 crewel needle
Dressmaker's tracing paper
Pincushion pattern (Fig 97)
Small amount of stuffing
Scraps of lightweight material, such as silk or satin, in a pastel shade to make a pad

Method

Trace Fig 97, adding an appropriate initial and the date to give a really personal touch if the pincushion is being made for a special occasion

Fig 96 Two pincushions and a christening invitation (worked by the author)

Fig 97 Pattern for square pincushion

such as an engagement or a wedding present. The one I made (Fig 96) was for my younger daughter's twenty-first birthday. This design would also make a delightful christening keepsake for a little girl, especially if the date of her baptism is embroidered on the back. Keepsakes were very popular in the nineteenth century, so by making and giving these little gifts we are keeping alive a lovely old custom.

Transfer the design to the material following the instructions given for transferring designs on p. 85. Work the embroidery using stem stitch for the stems and padded satin stitch for the leaves. The flower petals are worked as shown in Fig 64f and the centres are small eyelets.

When the embroidery is completed work running stitches on the sewing line (- - - -) (Fig 97). Trace the pincushion outline on the backing material and work running stitches around this line. Wash and press both pieces. Cut away surplus material to 3 mm from the sewing line on both front and back pieces. Fold the material under to the sewing line on back and front and join on three sides. With the pastel material make a pad, insert in the pincushion cover and stitch along the fourth side.

The second pincushion in Fig 96 would make an excellent sampler of needlepoint fillings. Trace off the pattern (Fig 98) and embroider using stem stitch, satin stitch, overcasting and eyelets. Work large eyelet fillings as described for Fig 79 and Fig 80. Work tiny buttonhole stitches close together around the lace edge. On the back piece of material mark a circle to fit the circle on the embroidered piece. Work running stitches around this line. Wash and press both pieces. Cut the embroidery from the foundation material very carefully. From the back piece, cut away the surplus material to 3 mm from the stitched circle. Fold the 3 mm under on the back piece and join to the front with tiny stitches for two thirds of the way round under the embroidered circle, being careful that the stitches do not show on the right side.

Fig 98 Pattern for needlepoint sampler pincushion

Make a pad to fit in a pastel shade of fine material such as silk or satin and insert. Stitch the remaining third of the opening and finish off securely.

The small initialled card (Fig 96) would make a charming 'New Baby' card or christening invitation. Draw and embroider an initial on fine cotton lawn, adding a flower to give it an Ayrshire needlework touch. Wash, press and cut from the foundation material. Using No. 100 lace thread, stitch to a scrap of lightweight material in a pastel shade. Set in a blank art card with a cut-out window, fold the flap over and secure in place with adhesive. To finish, add an appropriate message.

15 Caring for heirlooms

If we consider the treatment the old christening robes received in their infancy, it is surprising that so many have survived. Those who are lucky enough to possess a christening robe or a piece of Ayrshire needlework which has been handed down to them through the generations, and who hope to pass it on to future generations, should take care to ensure that it is stored and preserved in the best possible way.

Many of these inherited items are yellowed, creased and torn. Deterioration of the fabric may have already taken place and been accelerated by many local and general factors. Any fabric which is crushed or tightly folded will deteriorate more quickly along the crease iines, as stress is put on the fabric fibres in these areas. Frequent and rough handling can cause damage by introducing dirt and sweat between the fibres, as does a lot of wear. A plump baby squeezed into its ancestral inheritance can do a robe irreparable damage. Other destructive factors include frequent exposure to sunlight, storage conditions which are too dry or too moist, and atmospheric pollution by chemicals in industrial and city areas. Another cause of structural damage to the fibres is caused by careless treatment in the past, such as not rinsing out completely all the chemicals and starch used in the laundering of the garment. This shows up as tiny holes which are often mistakenly blamed on moths.

Anyone who possesses an Ayrshire needlework robe should examine it with certain reservations before making a decision on how best to maintain and preserve it. It may be torn and have worn areas, or some of the needlelace fillings may be completely destroyed. Repair of the fabric or seams can be carried out by a competent needlewoman, but repair to the actual embroidery requires a practised working knowledge of the craft. When patching, material of a similar weight and a very fine needle and thread must be used.

A successful and almost invisible patch can be obtained by the following method, which is a combination of patching and darning. The material surrounding the area to be patched must be in good condition. Cut the new fabric about 5 cm to 7 cm larger in each direction than the area to be replaced. Keeping the grain running in the same direction, pin the new fabric in place on the right side. Turn to the back and, taking a tacking thread through both layers, mark the damaged area which is to be covered by the patch. Return to the right side. Withdraw threads from the surplus material on the patch to the tacked line, along one side. Darn each thread singly out from the tacked line for 1.5 cm to 2.5 cm. The quickest way to do this is to insert the needle where the darning thread is to go; separate the next free thread on the patch, thread the needle with it and pull it through. Repeat on the other three sides. Cut off all the ends and press. A tiny repair using this method can be seen in one of the working samplers in Fig 54.

If professional help is sought, the resulting financial cost should first be taken into consideration, as it may be greater than the value of the garment. Sentimental value must, of course, also be taken into account.

Once the item has been repaired it must be cleaned. If it is very fragile and worn, again professional help should be sought. Most museums, if they do not have their own conservator, are willing to give advice as to where help can be obtained. Modern biological powders tend to contain bleaching agents and, although an old article may appear to be greatly improved after washing with one of these powders, if not completely removed, the bleaching agent may cause deterioration in the fibres of the fabric. Remember, an intact yellowed robe is usually more interesting than a repaired and abused brilliant white one.

The fabric becomes heavier when wet, so larger items such as christening robes should be supported throughout the wash, for example in a net bag of the kind used for washing tights, or one made from an old, clean, white net curtain. If there are stains whose cause is known, modern stain removers produced for specific stains may be used with great care. Use only a dabbing action; the stain must not be rubbed, as this will damage the fabric.

Place the robe in the net bag and soak in several changes of cold water. Handle very carefully and do not wring. Choose a good quality washing powder which contains no bleaching agent. Thoroughly dissolve the washing powder in one gallon of hot water in accordance with the instructions on the packet and allow to cool. Half fill a large pan from this solution – I use my preserving pan. Immerse the robe, bring it slowly to the boil and boil very gently for five to ten minutes. You should only just be able to see movement in the water. Tip the robe into the sink and rinse under gently running cold water. Using fresh washing powder solution, repeat the boiling process. This time rinse thoroughly in several changes of hand-hot water, and finally in cold water. Personally I prefer to use the old method of boiling so that the water gently percolates through the fibres of the material, rather than lifting the garment in and out of the water, prodding and agitating it. Where there are problems with hard water, err on the safe side and use distilled water.

If a starched garment is wanted for a baptism, use a good quality starch at this stage and follow the instructions on the packet. Remember the starch must be thoroughly rinsed out of the garment after it has been used. It also has to be pressed, as it must never be put away creased. Gently squeeze out as much surplus water as possible and carefully remove the robe from the net bag. Spread out on a large dye-free towel or bath sheet. Place another towel on top and fold double. Leave for about thirty minutes. If too much water is retained repeat the process with two dry towels.

While it is still damp, iron the robe on the reverse side, taking great care that the iron is not too hot. The bodice is the most difficult area to iron. To make this task easier the nineteenth-century launderess had a small iron, about 10 cm long, which was made specially for the purpose and called a 'bodice iron'. I find it very difficult and cumbersome to work on such a small area with a normal iron so I substitute my little travelling iron, which is ideal.

It is not the wearing of the robe for a baptism which damages it, but rather the preparation of the garment for the ceremony and the laundering afterwards. I am often shown robes in a very crumpled condition, the excuse for which is that the owners are afraid they will damage the fabric if they iron it, whereas the opposite is in fact true.

Recently I was bequeathed a collection of Ayrshire needlework. The Trustees who delivered it were of the opinion that it was only fit for the dustbin. The articles were so ingrained with over a hundred years of smoke and dust, that they soiled anything with which they came into contact. After being laundered by the above method, they became treasures of rare beauty. Now that they have been properly stored I hope they will survive and give much pleasure for the next hundred years.

Constant storage conditions are easier to produce if the items are boxed. To store your Ayrshire needlework, prepare a clean box which is large enough to hold the items with as little folding as possible. Suitable boxes can often be obtained from florists. Each item should be loosely layered with white acid-free tissue paper to support the article, and then more tissue paper placed over the surface to protect it. Even the tiny buttons on robes should be padded to prevent them from pressing against and damaging another area. It is essential that items are not put under any pressure by squeezing too many into one box. A handkerchief can be laid flat with acid-free tissue paper on either side and a small bonnet carefully stuffed with crushed tissue paper to ensure it retains its shape. Acid-free tissue paper is usually available from good stationery suppliers. Use white tissue paper, as the coloured variety is not dyefast. Articles should never be placed in plastic bags, as these can induce high humidity levels, leaving damp patches on the material which may lead to mildew staining.

Once the needlework is boxed, the lid should be labelled with the contents, giving a detailed description of each item so that the box need not be opened more frequently than necessary. This prevents over-handling of the articles or changes in atmospheric conditions inside the box, therefore leading to better preservation.

The box should be stored out of sunlight, ideally at a constant temperature of 13–14 degrees Centigrade and at a humidity of around 55%. This is easily obtained in museums, where air-conditioned storage can be created to produce the best environment, but is not always possible in the home, so reasonable care must be taken, keeping the articles boxed, clean and away from heat, damp and sunlight, if they are to be preserved for future generations.

A great deal of interest can be added if you photograph and document your collection. Photograph each baby baptised in your robe and remember to add his or her name, christening and birth details to it afterwards. If a handkerchief has been made for a bride, add the date of the wedding, details of the bride and groom and the embroideress to the documentation. The autographs of all the guests add a charming and interesting touch for posterity. How I wish all the pieces in my collection had been documented or could tell their story. Were they made with love, hope and expectancy, or were they the result of sweated labour, with the additional price of eyesight and ill health?

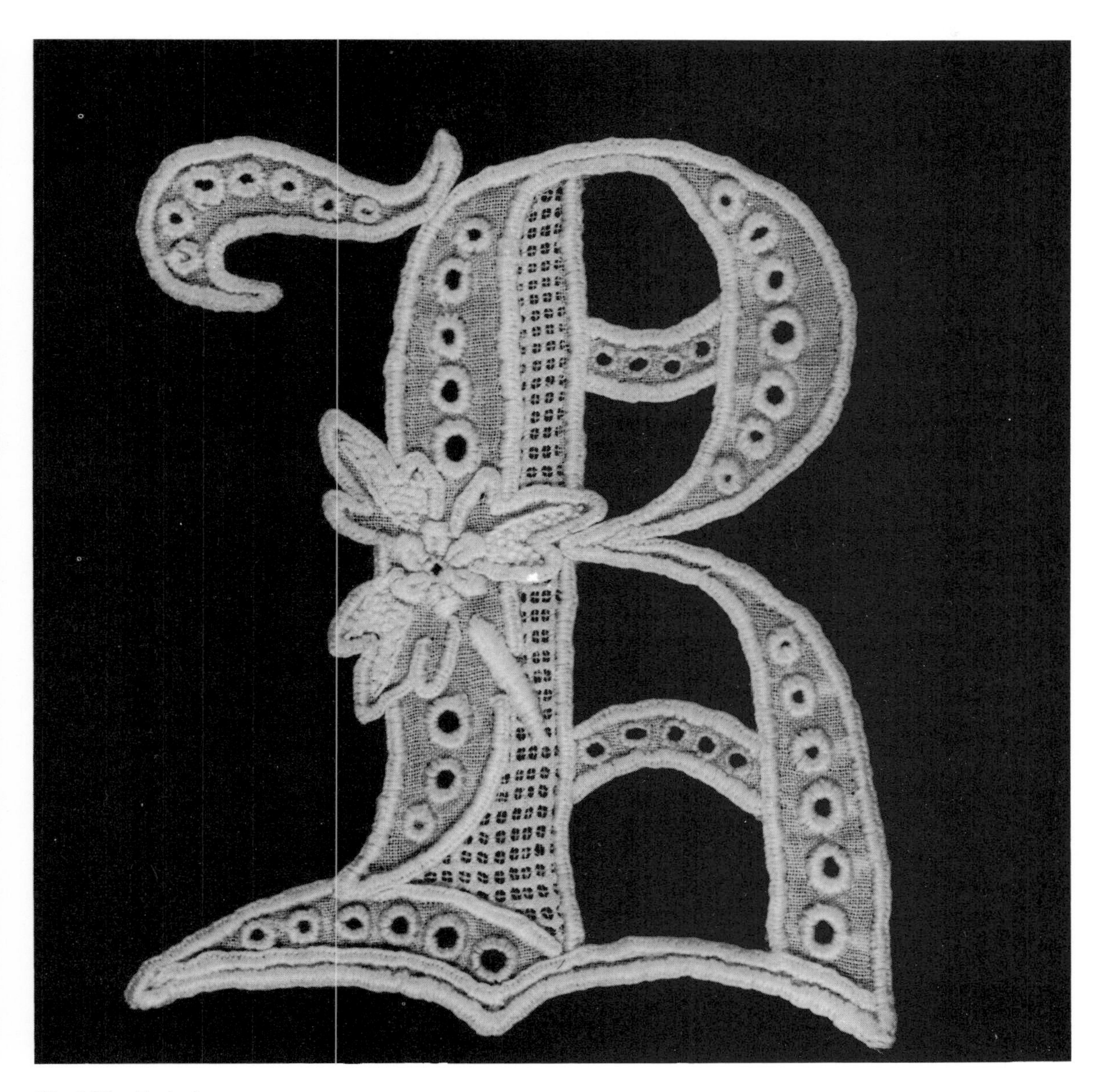

Fig 105 End piece

Fig 99 Designs for Ayrshire needlework

Fig 100 Designs for Ayrshire needlework

Fig 101 Designs for Ayrshire needlework

Fig 102 Designs for Ayrshire needlework

Fig 103 Designs for Ayrshire needlework

Fig 104 Designs for Ayrshire needlework

Embroidery collections

Scotland

The Baird Institute Museum
Cumnock
Ayrshire
Open Friday 9.30 am–1 pm and 1.30 pm–4 pm. Saturday 11 am–1 pm. Permission to view at other times can be arranged by writing to the District Council Office, Lugar, Ayrshire

Blair Castle
Blair Atholl
Perthshire
Open Easter week and every day from 1 April until the last Friday in October

Dean Castle
Kilmarnock
Scotland
Small display on show daily from 12 am–5 pm

Dick Institute
Kilmarnock
Scotland
Small display which can be seen during Museum opening hours
April to September, Monday, Tuesday, Thursday, Friday, 10 am–8pm
Wednesday and Saturday 10 am–5 pm (closed Sundays)
October to March Monday to Saturday 10 am–5pm

Glasgow Museum & Art Galleries
Kelvingrove
Glasgow G3 8AG
Excellent collection. For appointment to view, apply to the Director, tel 041 357 3929

Kyle & Carrick District Library & Museum Services
12 Main Street
Ayr
For permission to view, apply to the Director of Libraries and Museums

Museums & Galleries
Rozelle
Alloway
Ayrshire
Collection can be seen by arrangement with the Director

Paisley Museum
High Street
Paisley
Collection not often on display, but can be seen by appointment

Royal Museum of Edinburgh
National Museums of Scotland
Chambers Street
Edinburgh Tel: 031 225 7534
Apply to Director for permission to view

England

Gawthorpe Hall
Padiham
Near Burnley
Lancs

Victoria and Albert Museum
South Kensington
London SW7

The Embroiderers' Guild
Apartment 41
Hampton Court Palace
East Molesey
Surrey KT8 9AU
Collection available to members of the Embroiderers' Guild: apply to Curator

Ireland

Ulster Museum
Botanic Gardens
Belfast BT9 5AB

New Zealand

National Museum of New Zealand
PO Box 467
Wellington
New Zealand

Tasmania

Van Dieman's Land Memorial Folk Museum
Narryna
103 Hampden Road
Hobart 7000
Tasmania

Suppliers

Liberty's of London
(Shops throughout UK)

Needlecraft
201 King Street
Castle Douglas
Kirkcudbrightshire
Scotland
Tel: 0556 3606
(Supplier of fine cotton lawn)

Jenny A'Things
3 Lainshaw Street
Stewarton
Ayrshire
Tel: 0560 84113
(Supplier of fine cotton lawn)

Christine Riley
53 Barclay Street
Stonehaven
Kincardineshire AB3 2AR

The Embroidery Shop
57 William Street
Edinburgh EH3 7LW

The Royal School of Needlework
5 King Street
Covent Garden
London WC2 8HN
Tel: 01 240 3186/7/8
(Conservators)

Peter & Beverly Scarlett
Strupak
Coldwells
Ellon
Aberdeenshire AB4 9YX
(Lace threads)

Impress Cards
Slough Farm
Westhall
Halesworth
Suffolk IP19 8RN

Index

Figures in italics refer to illustrations